CREDIT SECRETS

THE BEST TRICKS AND SECRETS TO REPAIR YOUR CREDIT AND IMPROVE YOUR SCORE. CHANGE YOUR FINANCIAL LIFE. MANAGE YOUR EXPENSES AND MONEY IN A SIMPLE AND EFFECTIVE WAY IN TIMES OF CRISIS

Tony Risk

© Copyright 2021 by Tony Risk - All rights reserved.

The following Book is reproduced below with the goal of providing information that is as accurate and reliable as possible. Regardless, purchasing this Book can be seen as consent to the fact that both the publisher and the author of this book are in no way experts on the topics discussed within and that any recommendations or suggestions that are made herein are for entertainment purposes only. Professionals should be consulted as needed prior to undertaking any of the action endorsed herein.

This declaration is deemed fair and valid by both the American Bar Association and the Committee of Publishers Association and is legally binding throughout the United States.

Furthermore, the transmission, duplication, or reproduction of any of the following work including specific information will be considered an illegal act irrespective of if it is done electronically or in print. This extends to creating a secondary or tertiary copy of the work or a recorded copy and is only allowed with the express written consent from the Publisher. All additional right reserved.

The information in the following pages is broadly considered a truthful and accurate account of facts and as such, any inattention, use, or misuse of the information in question by the reader will render any resulting actions solely under their purview. There are no scenarios in which the publisher or the original author of this work can be in any fashion deemed liable for any hardship or damages that may befall them after undertaking information described herein.

Additionally, the information in the following pages is intended only for informational purposes and should thus be thought of as universal. As befitting its nature, it is presented without assurance regarding its prolonged validity or interim quality. Trademarks that are mentioned are done without written consent and can in no way be considered an endorsement from the trademark holder.

Table Of Contents

INTRODUCTION 6

CHAPTER 1: WHAT IS THE CREDIT SCORE? 8

CHAPTER 2: HOW CREDIT SCORE IS DETERMINED 12
- WHAT KIND OF CREDIT DO YOU HAVE? 12
- BUILDING UP CREDIT 13
- THE MYTH OF PAYING IT OFF 14

CHAPTER 3: WHY SHOULD I CARE ABOUT HAVING GOOD CREDIT? ... 16
- POOR PEOPLE PAY MORE FEES 16

CHAPTER 4: WHEN YOU FIND YOURSELF WITH BAD CREDIT? 20
- WHAT IS BAD CREDIT? 20
- WHEN SHOULD YOU WORRY? 20
- HOW CREDIT CARDS CAN CAUSE BAD CREDIT 21
- WHAT YOU SHOULD KNOW ABOUT CREDIT CARD DEBT 21

CHAPTER 5: WHAT IS IN A CREDIT REPORT? 26
- INVESTIGATIVE REPORTS 31
- WHO CAN LOOK AT YOUR CREDIT REPORT? 32

CHAPTER 6: THE RIGHT WAY TO CHECK YOUR CREDIT REPORT .. 38
- WHERE TO OBTAIN YOUR CREDIT REPORT 38
- HOW OFTEN ARE YOU ALLOWED A FREE COPY OF YOUR CREDIT REPORT? . 39
- YOUR 6-STEP CREDIT CHECK CHECKLIST 39
- THE 2 THINGS YOU MUST DO IF YOU FIND ERRORS ON YOUR CREDIT REPORT 41
- 5 BONUS TIPS 43

CHAPTER 7: TEN CREDIT SCORE MYTHS TO UNLEARN 46

CHAPTER 8: WHAT'S A GOOD CREDIT SCORE? 54
- UNDERSTANDING FICO CREDIT SCORE 55
- HOW FICO SCORES HELP YOU 56
- HOW TO OBTAIN A GOOD CREDIT SCORE 58

CHAPTER 9: HOW TO USE AND FIX IDENTITY THEFT 66

    HOW IDENTITY THEFT HAPPENS 67
    WHAT TO DO IF YOU ARE A VICTIM OF IDENTITY THEFT 69
    PROTECTING YOURSELF FROM IDENTITY THEFT 73

CHAPTER 10: THE RIGHT MINDSET 76

    THE GOOD DEBT 78
    WHAT IS BAD DEBT? 81
    USING CONSOLIDATION OR SETTLEMENT STRATEGIES TO PAY DOWN DEBTS
    82
    NEGOTIATE WITH CREDIT COMPANIES 83
    CUT THE CREDIT CARDS 84
    TALKING TO CREDITORS 85

CHAPTER 11: THE IMPORTANCE OF A GOOD CREDIT SCORE 86

    WHY IS YOUR CREDIT SCORE IMPORTANT? 86
    STARTING FROM THE SCRATCH AND MAINTAINING IT 89
    HOW TO BUILD A CREDIT SCORE FROM SCRATCH? 90
    CREDIT REPAIR: HOW TO IMPROVE YOUR CREDIT SCORE 93
    CHECK THE CREDIT REPORT 94

CHAPTER 12: YOUR FINANCIAL FREEDOM 102

    CREDIT CARDS AND FINANCIAL FREEDOM - IS IT SAFE? 103
    THE BEST HABITS TO HELP YOU REACH AND PROTECT YOUR FINANCIAL
    FREEDOM 104

CONCLUSION 110

TONY RISK

Introduction

A credit score is simply an endeavor to rank your creditworthiness with a goal number. It used to be that in the event that you needed a credit, you would go into the bank; and in the event that you had a decent remaining in the network, or if the advance official had a positive sentiment about you, you could get an advance. Clearly, there is a blemish in that framework; anyone, regardless of how very much regarded, can be an awful credit hazard. Along these lines, by computing the impact of various factors on your capacity to reimburse, the credit offices concocted a way that tries to treat everyone decently.

There are a few distinct things considered by the credit offices when making sense of a score. Fortunately, a large portion of them is good judgment. The one thing that makes up the majority of your score is your installment history. Along these lines, probably the best thing you can begin doing (or keep doing) is to take care of the entirety of your tabs on schedule. Next, don't owe excessively. Your obligation to-salary proportion ought to be at 25% or less. That implies the sum you owe ought not to surpass 25% of your pay. Try not to open such a large number of records in a brief timeframe, and don't lose an excessive amount of either. Possibly, apply for an advance or credit in the event that you genuinely need it. As referenced, a large portion of these things are sound judgment, and they will consistently go far towards improving your general budgetary wellbeing.

Is a credit score actually that significant, all things considered, it's just a number, isn't that so? Right, however, it's an inescapable number at that. The most notable model is the banks. They will utilize your credit score to decide if you get an advance, and assuming this is the case, what terms you will get. Be that as it may, your credit score is utilized by much something other than moneylenders. On the off chance that you go after a position, your potential business may pull your credit report before settling on their employing choice. Proprietors use credit scores to see who they will lease to. Insurance agencies use them as a component of their hazard evaluation before offering you an arrangement.

There is no uncertainty that your credit score is significant. Since you have more data on what it's everything about, you can find a way to maintain or improve your score.

Truth be told, learning about credit and finance can be an intimidating task, I believe one should seek to understand anything they choose to participate in, and to be honest, we don't have a choice when it comes to credit. Why not have the knowledge and understanding of credit; regardless of any trade or career you are in or will pursue, credit can always be used as a tool of leverage no matter how much money you have or make. Pay attention to how even the wealthy people secure mortgages to purchase their property and pay interest while still building equity.

CHAPTER 1:

What Is The Credit Score?

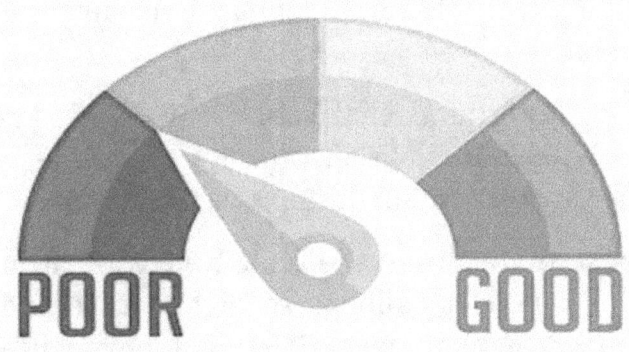

Credit is a broad term in the financial world that has many different meanings. The idea of credit is nothing new, and it is some sort or another that most people have used. What is credit, then?

It is generally defined as a contractual agreement whereby a borrower receives something of value and agrees to pay back the lender at a later date — generally with interest. Often, it might even include, for example, crediting a 401(k).

Credit also refers to an individual or company's creditworthiness, or credit history. It also refers to an accounting entry that either reduces assets or increases liabilities and equity on the balance sheet of a company.

If you're paying back those friendly loans, you're building trust with your parents, friends, or anyone else who lends you money. This trust helps build your reputation and increase your future borrowing chances.

This is the same concept used by financial institutions, such as banks when determining whether to extend credit to you or not. Such firms analyze your credit report and use your history to decide whether or not they will lend you money, how much, and at what cost. The higher the credit score, the greater the likelihood that you will earn a loan and, usually, the lower the interest rate.

There is no uncertainty that your credit score is significant. Since you have more data on what it's everything about, you can find a way to maintain or improve your score.

If you get several loans at the same time while using a credit card, then your debt balloons so high that you will end up having no capacity to pay. Even if a few obligations are discharged, you find it impossible to pay them all.

Let's assume that you did manage to get rid of all your debt somehow. You finally get the courage to apply for a credit card. Sadly, the bank rejected your application, so you applied for another. Still, you got rejected and you finally noticed the problem — your credit score.

Before a bank gives you a credit card, they think about your financial behavior. Banks run a risk assessment to be sure that you'll pay back what you borrowed. Being responsible with credit is a deciding factor for you to get an approved application.

For quick reference, banks use credit scores to assess you. A credit score is a three-figure grade given to consumers that measure their creditworthiness or ability to pay back the amount borrowed.

Your credit score, since it is a quantitative basis of your debt, needs to be based on real information about your financial history. A credit report is the primary resource of credit scores, which we will tackle in detail later.

The FICO score from the Fair Isaac Corporation is the usual credit score that most lenders use. The FICO score ranges from 300 to 850 with a higher score implying creditworthiness.

Although the FICO score has been used for over 20 years as a reliable resource, it is not the deciding factor in your loan application. Each bank has its own set of criteria for granting debt to clients.

CHAPTER 2:

How Credit Score Is Determined

Having bad credit affects not just what you want now, but also what you can have in years to come. Your credit score will affect everything from hire purchasing to getting a mortgage. That is why it is vital you keep any good credit that you have and keep the bad credit ratings away.

Bad credit ratings generally come from missed payments on things such as loans, mortgages, and credit card payments. To sum it all up, bad credit comes from any time that you don't pay back any money that you have borrowed from banks, building societies, or other lenders.

What Kind of Credit Do You Have?

Are you in the so-called 'prime sector,' the 40% of the population that has an excellent credit rating? If you miss one mortgage repayment, you may drop a point or two, but overall, it will not affect your credit rating.

You can see that most people aren't in this group. 60% of us are in the sub-prime sector with a less than perfect credit score. The way in which your credit rating is scored varies greatly when you are in this group. If you miss a payment on your mortgage, you may drop 20 points on your credit score; if you miss a payment on your credit card, you may lose more.

But just imagine: If you were in the prime sector of ratings, you may not drop any points whatsoever. That might not sound fair, but it's true. Also, there is no way to know for sure how many points you will drop for missing payments. It's completely unpredictable, and you never know exactly what is happening.

That is why you need to read this book!

Credit company bosses are getting fat on the profits you give them in interest payments each month. Don't let that happen! That is why you should never have more debt than a quarter of what you earn per year. This way you can be sure you can make the payments on time. Other than a mortgage or maybe a business loan, you should never get yourself into any more debt for whatever reason. Remember: Any such debt will hang around your neck for months, maybe even years.

Building Up Credit

If you need to build up credit because you don't have any, or because you have extremely bad credit, then you need a plan to get back on the right track. Pretty much everything you do in your life affects your credit rating, even things that you would never imagine. This includes things such as:

- How much car insurance you pay
- How much house insurance you pay
- How you pay your insurance bills
- Possibly, even health insurance.

Even your job can also affect your credit rating more than you would think.

The Myth of Paying It Off

If you have no credit but you manage to get a credit card, do you think it is better to pay the balance all off at once every month or pay it off in installments? Many people would say pay it off every month. After all, that way, you have no debt, pay no interest, and establish yourself as a reliable person, right?

But think about it: If you pay it off in full every month, you are effectively not borrowing any money; therefore, you do not have any score on your credit rating. If you pay the debt off in installments, you are building up your good credit rating — provided you make the minimum payment on time.

CHAPTER 3:

Why Should I Care About Having Good Credit?

No matter what race you are, where you were born, where you live, or who your parents are, it doesn't even matter what occupation you are in, your name in itself is worth money. How much money your name will be worth is solely up to you, your thinking and the knowledge you pursue. I always tell people I don't care if you are homeless or even fresh out of prison, if you have nothing else as far as assets or money to your name, you were born into a system where numbers can equal money. The numbers I'm referring to are your social security number. On paper in this country, we are all born the same, we all have clean slates and no social security number meaning anything greater than the next generated set of numbers. This is a very logical and productive way of thinking; no need to fall into conspiracy theories or feel inferior, the structure of your existence on paper is that of an entity that is fresh and undetermined, it will be up to you how you use it. How much do you want your signature to be worth?

Poor People Pay More Fees

Just as taxes are more favorable to the rich because of loopholes and write-offs, the same kind of advantages can exist in the credit world. Money is not what separates classes of people, it's information and resources. Those who are well-off have access to more information; and with better credit, they qualify for the lowest interest rates. The higher the credit score, the cheaper it will be to borrow money and to finance bigger purchases like mortgages. Take note of the payday lenders, sub-prime credit card issuers, and reloadable debit cards that are marketed only to those who lack the information to seek better financial products. We have predatory auto lenders with sky-high interest rates that will finance almost anyone with a nose on their face regardless of their credit. These lenders target those with very little financial education and options; the people who take these offers just need to fulfill a short-term need and can careless about calculating an interest rate. Pay attention to where you see most of these companies and their advertisements.

Half of the adults in America do not have $1,000 in their savings account; and besides having no financial education, poor people are unfairly targeted by payday lenders and check-cashing establishments. These companies infest neighborhoods with higher poverty rates, mostly filled with minorities. Wherever you find the uneducated, you will find major institutions ready to take advantage of these same people. Yes, payday lenders target the vulnerable, and this is no secret as it has become a part of everyday business. Go to any city in this country and you will find payday loan businesses that offer money at an annual percentage rate of 390%. Even if you paid someone to fix your credit, it would still cost less than the fees you will pay on one of these kinds of loans. Why would anyone pay these rates? They either gave up on their credit or just lack the right information and don't know they are being ripped off.

A $1,000 loan would cost you over $4,000 to pay back within a year, legal loan sharking at its finest. Only those who have no available credit or access to borrow money in a traditional sense will accept a loan shark offer like this. For someone who is already making minimum wage or struggling from week to week, getting an advance on your next paycheck is financial suicide as the rates are never affordable. It isn't much of a need for a check cashing establishment on every corner in the suburbs. 11 million people use payday loan services each year; and the average person will pay close to $500 in fees in addition to the loan, think about that for a minute. Western Union, MoneyGram, check cashing, title loan, and payday loan businesses are offered 3 to 4 times more in the poverty sections of our cities versus in the affluent or better sides of town.

Where do normal people learn the ends and outs of the credit system? How many working-class people have heard of ChexSystems? Most people think that if they become delinquent on a bank account, the activity will show up on their credit reports, not true. The average person is oblivious to how to go about checking any of their consumer reports; some don't even realize all of these companies even exist. The system is not meant to be simple or transparent; the most valuable thing on earth is information, and nobody is in a rush to educate you.

10 Basic Reasons to Have Good Credit

1. Get funds to start or grow your business.

2. You will have access to money for emergencies.

3. You can qualify to buy a home and build equity.

4. Borrow unsecured money for college.

5. Access to reward programs that offer free travel.

6. Zero or low-interest auto loans.

7. No deposits on utilities and some leases.

8. Qualify for job opportunities that require decent credit and save thousands on insurance policies each year.

9. Purchase protection from merchants.

10. Travel protection and zero liability rental car insurance.

CHAPTER 4:

When You Find Yourself With Bad Credit?

What Is Bad Credit?

We often hear the phrase "bad credit" and are told our credit is bad, but we are never directly told what it actually means. In general, bad credit is a score that tells people what your potential is for paying back debt in full and on time. Bad credit is based on your previous history of paying off debt. It takes a look at if you paid off a bill in full if you made payments, and if you were on time.

There are several forms of debt that are reported to show up on your credit report from automobile loans, home loans, student loans, and credit cards. If you have ever looked up your credit score, you will understand everything that is a part of your score and what it says.

When Should You Worry?

You realize, through your history, that your main problem is your credit card debt.

While I will get into this later, it is important to state now that when you should worry is never as worry will only lead you to have a negative mindset and can cause physical problems that will not help your situation. I understand this is easier said than done, which is one reason I focus on having the right mindset, but you have to understand that worry is not going to help you overcome credit card debt, and it will not assist you in reaching financial freedom.

Therefore, instead of asking when you should worry, you should ask yourself what you can do to overcome your credit card debt and delete bad credit.

How Credit Cards Can Cause Bad Credit

Some people feel that if they take out a couple of credit cards and make the minimum payment every month, they will be able to build up their credit score. While this can help increase your credit score, it can also easily cause you to fall into having bad credit due to credit card debt. One of the main reasons credit cards cause bad credit is because people don't fully understand credit card debt and how it can impact your score.

What You Should Know About Credit Card Debt

People know the basics about credit cards. Once you are approved, you then receive your card and activate it. You can use it for pretty much anything, such as for purchasing groceries, clothing, or for paying bills. At the same time, you can also get a pin number for many credit cards which will allow you to head to an ATM to get some cash-out. The nice part is that you only have to make the minimum payment every month to keep yourself out of credit card debt. Unfortunately, it is this kind of thinking that often leads people into credit card debt.

Below are some basic points that most people don't realize about credit card debt.

1. Know when short-term loans make more sense

Sometimes we need to get some cash or find a way to pay a few bills quickly. Many people turn to credit cards for these reasons. They receive their answer within minutes and their card will arrive in the mail in about five to seven business days. However, sometimes it is better to go to your bank and talk to a loan advisor instead. If you need a couple of thousand dollars in order to pay off your medical bills so they don't get sent to a collection agency, it might be best to take out a short-term loan from your local bank or credit union. These loans usually take about six months to pay off and will help you repair your credit and keep you more financially free than any credit card.

2. Credit card debt can result in bad credit

Paying off your credit cards in a less than timely manner or missing the minimum payment aren't the only things that are going to result in you having bad credit; having credit cards that hold high balances can also increase your chances of bad credit. This is why it is important to never max out your credit cards. In fact, you should make sure you always have at least 30 percent of your credit limit available.

While it is almost impossible in today's world, your best chance of keeping yourself from having bad credit is by remaining as free of debt as you possibly can.

3. Owing is the easy part, and the hard part is paying credit cards back

The reality of life is that you never really know what is going to happen. You could have a job for a couple of decades and then find out that you are randomly laid off due to cutbacks. You could have an illness spike that causes surgery. There are a lot of situations that can cause you to think you can start paying your credit cards every other month so you can make other bills. You could also find yourself struggling to pay the full minimum balance, so you may decide to pay about half of it every month.

Another reason your debt will climb is due to your credit limit increasing. This makes you feel mentally secure about being able to purchase your new couch on your credit card because your limit just increased by $500. However, what you are really doing is creating more credit card debt and causing your minimum monthly payment to increase. On top of this, your interest is going to compound, which makes it increase.

4. You will find yourself spending more than you make

It doesn't matter how responsible you are with credit cards; one of the biggest reasons people find themselves in credit card debt is because they spend more than they make every month. Credit cards are very tempting because they provide you with the thought that you can just pay it back later or make smaller payments on the purchase every month. Although, in reality, you should never spend more than what your monthly income is.

5. Most people use credit cards to handle emergency situations

It is common for people to tell others that a credit card is only used for emergencies, but do you really keep in mind what a true emergency is? Most people live paycheck to paycheck. Therefore, when they see their checking account balance drop low and there are several days before their next payday, they will start to think about each purchase they make and wonder if they should use their credit card as it is considered an emergency or a need. The best step for you to take is to start slowly saving a part of your check and place it into an emergency fund account.

6. People think as long as they make the minimum payment, they will be fine

In reality, you always want to make sure you pay more than the minimum payment. Think of it this way: if you have a $75 minimum payment, at least 25 percent of what you pay is going to go toward interest and fees. This means that you are really only putting 75 percent of your payment toward paying off your debt. Depending on how much you owe, this could be a low amount. If you aren't careful, you could find yourself going over your credit limit, which means your credit card company will charge you their over-the-limit fee.

Furthermore, only paying the minimum payment is going to take you years to pay off. It really doesn't matter how low you feel your credit limit is versus how high you believe your minimum monthly payment is. It can still take at least a couple of years to pay off your debt, providing you stop using your credit card.

TONY RISK

CHAPTER 5:

What Is In A Credit Report?

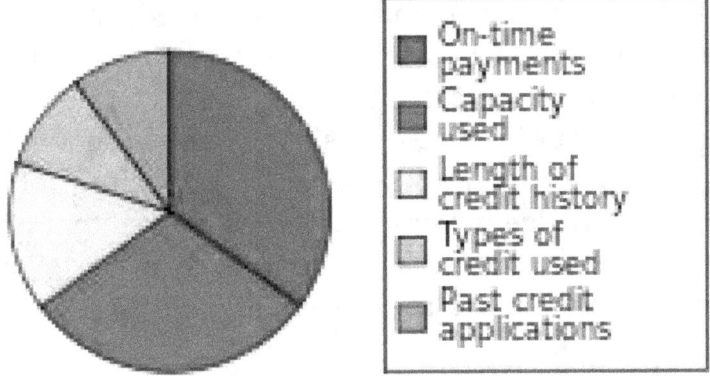

Information in your credit report can be broken down into five main categories:

- Personal information about you
- Accounts reported monthly
- Accounts reported when in default
- Public records
- Inquiries

Typically, most of the negative information in your credit file will remain there for seven years, but bankruptcies can remain there for up to ten years. Sometimes, credit reports separate and highlight the negative items in your credit report.

Some special credit reports contain even more information, called investigative reports. Credit reports do not contain race, religious preference, medical history, personal lifestyle, political preference, friends, or other non-credit-related information. Ordinary credit reports typically don't contain information about your income, investment, or bank accounts. Your credit report will contain information about you only, whether you are married, unmarried, divorced, or single. Your spouse's information should only appear in your report if both of you are allowed to use it and are required to pay an account. Information about joint accounts, for example, should appear on credit reports from both spouses. Your credit history is the source of knowledge in your credit report. Creditors typically use automated systems and standardized terms to pass on consumer account information to credit reporting agencies.

1. Personal Information

Credit reporting agencies collect this information from borrowers who receive it from you every time you complete a credit application. It's very important for that reason that your credit applications are accurate, complete, and legible.

2. Accounts Reported Monthly

The credit report on each of these accounts will typically contain the following information:

- Name of the creditor (which may be the original creditor or another creditor to whom the account has been transferred, including a transfer to the debt collector)

- Account type (e.g., mortgage or revolving)
- Account number
- When the account has been opened
- Your responsibility on the account (e.g. individual, authorized user, or joint account)
- The credit history — that is, for each invoice within the most recent 24 to 48 months, whether you paid on time or 30, 60, 90, or 120 days late; whether the account was "loaded off" or put for recovery, and the date on which the delinquency began; whether the account was assigned to a collection agency; whether the account was dismissed in bankruptcy; whether you dispose of the account; or whether you are disputing any charges
- The credit cap or the original loan sum
- Your present balance
- Your total balance on revolving accounts; Keep in mind as you review your report that your balance may not appear as zero, even if you pay your account in full each month. This is because the outstanding balance listed is probably the amount that you owed during the month before paying the balance at the end of the billing period.

Creditors who provide monthly reports generally include:

- Banks, savings and loans, credit unions, finance companies, and other commercial borrowers offering credit cards and making mortgage, family, auto, and student loans
- Nonbank credit and debit card issuers (such as American Express and Diners Club)

- Large department stores
- Oil and gas companies
- Other creditors accepting monthly installment fees on a regular basis.

3. Accounts Reported When in Default

Some firms only provide credit reporting agencies with details when an account is due past or the trustee has taken action against you, like handing the debt over to a collection agency. Generally, your credit report will include the following in these situations:

- Borrower identity (which may be the initial borrower or another creditor to whom the account has been passed, including the transition to the debt collector)
- Account form
- Account number
- Account obligation (e.g. person, registered holder, or joint account)
- The delinquency record — whether you are 60, 90, or 120 days late; whether the credit was "turned off" or put for recovery, and the day the delinquency began; whether the debt was assigned to a collection agency; whether you were sued; or whether the account was dismissed in bankruptcy.

Creditors who generally report accounts only when they are past due or in collection include:

- Landlords and property managers
- Utility companies

- Local retailers
- Insurance companies
- Magazines and newspapers
- Doctors and hospitals
- Lawyers and other professionals.

While creditors tend to report these accounts only when they're due past, credit reporting agencies are increasingly gathering monthly information from utilities, telephone companies, and local retailers to add to credit reports. The aim is to increase the data contained in individual files, such as young people and immigrants, who have little traditional credit history.

4. Public Records

Government agencies maintain public documents and are accessible to anyone. Public records are local, national, and federal court files. Federal law also requires credit reporting agencies to report offenses in child support submitted by enforcement agencies for child support.

5. Inquiries

The last details in your credit report are considered "inquiries." These are the lists of borrowers and others (such as a potential employer) who submitted a copy of your record during the year or two before. There are typically two types of collateral inquiries. The first type includes questions that only show up on the report you read, not on the report creditors get. There are several types of requests in this area, including creditors requiring your credit report for promotional purposes (think of all those pre-approved credit card applications you get in the mail), new creditors checking your report to verify you regularly, and reviews when you have received a copy of your own credit report. These are often referred to as gentle investigations. They have no bearing on your credit score.

These inquiries — often called "hard" inquiries — consist of investors who have asked for your report after you have negotiated with them for payment. For their impact on your credit score, please see below.

Investigative Reports

Some special credit reports have even more personal information than regular credit reports, called investigative reports. The big difference is that they include the character knowledge, general image, personal characteristics, or lifestyle obtained from interviews with third parties like your neighbors or friends. Creditors typically do not pay for these investigative reports. Insurers and companies are the most likely to ask about them. Because that information is confidential and intrusive, these records are subject to additional regulations. If a company or individual is asking for an investigative report, it must:

- Have a legitimate reason to seek a report

- Tell you, in writing, that you have the right to request a summary of the nature and scope of the investigation

- Reveal the nature and scope of the investigation if you request such material

- In certain cases, receive your permission. (For example, companies that procure employees for prospective employers, such as headhunters, must obtain the consent of the consumer before conducting the investigation and again before reporting the results to the employer.) However, if an employer requests a report to investigate misconduct or infringements of the law of the employee (instead of creditworthiness, standing, or capacity), he does not have to give you advice.

Who Can Look at Your Credit Report?

You might be shocked by the organizations and entities that are permitted to check your credit report and are constantly doing so. The Federal Fair Credit Reporting Act (FCRA) (15 U.S.C. Section 1681 and subsequent) and state credit reporting statutes limit who can read and use the credit report. Any organization or entity that demands your credit report shall be controlled by the FCRA. The individuals and organizations that may qualify for your credit report include:

- Although this is a broad category, certain limitations do exist. You must have made a bid or otherwise launched a payment agreement for a new transaction before the borrower can look at the paper. It is important to be careful when shopping around, especially when it comes to cars. Dealers will try to get you to sign an agreement before they launch their sales pitch, so they can look at your documents and size up the financial situation. That letter will then show in your credit report and could have a negative impact on your score.

- Mortgage lenders can be trusted to scrutinize your study very closely before offering to give you money to buy a house. If you are looking to borrow $150,000 or more, the lender will be given older records. But mortgage lenders often see details which other investors would not get.

- Landlords, who may receive a report from a specialist consumer reporting agency monitoring rental records, including expulsions.

- Utility companies that are able to request your credit report. In many cases, however, there are often state rules that prevent utility companies from refusing you service, even if you have bad credit. In general, negative marks should only matter if you owe money to the particular utility company that you are seeking service from. Even then, most energy companies are required to offer low-income people special payment plans and services that allow them to get subsidized utility services.

- Student borrowers. As of July 1, 2010, federal loans are made directly by the government — there are no private lenders offering them. Generally speaking, a direct federal student loan can't be denied depending on your net value. Yet parents eligible for PLUS loans will be tested for the cash. Remember, if you are in default on another federal loan, you cannot get a new federal loan unless you have made appropriate plans for repaying it. Nevertheless, private student loan borrowers (those not offered by the government) can use credit reports for making loans or tracking existing loans.

- Insurance companies that can look at your documents when you are paying for a contract. They are usually not interested in your credit history but may ask about your medical history or any insurance claims you have filed. If you are looking for $150,000 or more in life insurance, the life insurance company is entitled to see older information that would otherwise not be included in your credit report

- Car insurance companies that frequently use credit information to help determine how much to charge when a new policy is offered. For example, according to

GMAC Insurance, insurers focus on studies that show "a very strong correlation between the financial history of a client and the probability of insurance claims in the future."

- Employers. Tens of thousands of employers are reviewing credit reports as part of assessing job applicants. Employers must first request your written authorization and provide other reports before ordering your credit report. Deciding whether to authorize a client to get your credit report leaves a lot of staff and job applicants in a contractual role. If you say no, you might look like you're hiding something and turning yourself down for the job. When you say yes and the interviewer does not like what he sees, then you have the right to see the paper and challenge any inaccuracies before being disqualified for the job. (In some jurisdictions, a copy of your credit report can be accessed at the same time as the contractor does.) But what if the information is correct? The best you can do is claim your problems are behind you and have little or no impact on performance at work. Nonetheless, keep in mind that many employers never look at credit reports. And those who do still won't care about your financial issues. If you have some negative information about your work, you may want to speak to the boss about it before they see the paper. If you are seeking a job that pays $75,000 or more, older information may be included in a credit report. So, if you agree to allow the employer to view your credit report, it may contain information other people won't see.

- Government agencies which may request your credit report to determine if you are eligible for public aid. They do this to seek hidden income or assets, not to see if you have bills that are unpaid. The law also allows officials from the state and local government to get reports to help determine if, and how much, you can pay in child support if they give you a 10 days' notice. When you apply for a license issued by a government agency, if it has to consider your financial status in deciding your eligibility, it can look into your credit report. But not every government agency can look into your credit report. District attorneys, for example, cannot look at findings that prosecute criminal or civil litigation, and the U.S. Citizenship and Immigration Services (formerly the INS) cannot request a reference for an immigration case or for reviewing applicants for citizenship. However, government agencies investigating international terrorism are allowed to obtain credit reports. Government agencies may also obtain credit reporting agencies' identifying information about you, such as name, address, former addresses, places of work, or former places of employment even if they do not have a credit-related purpose, eligibility for services, or child support.

Collection companies that can dig into your documents while trying to collect your unpaid debt. They do this mainly to try to locate you or to learn more about your assets.

- Decision creditors who wish to recover debt on the grounds of a financial transaction involving a normal borrower are entitled to look at credit reports and determine whether to commence recovery operation against you. They can also locate you or your assets using reports. At least one court has said that people who do not offer credit on a regular basis cannot get credit reports and try to collect a verdict, but other courts are not in agreement. This means that people may also be entitled to get a credit report and pay on a judgment in certain jurisdictions (for example, an alimony judgment or child support judgment).

- Entities having court rulings. Even if a person, agency, or business has no other permissible reason to get your report, it may get your report if it can get a court order (not easy to do). For example, the IRS might receive a summons that would allow you to access your credit report. Generally, you'd have notice and an opportunity to object to a court order request.

Most other people and businesses, apart from those listed above, cannot legally request a copy of your credit report. It's not always easy to find out whether someone who is not supposed to have access to your credit report has sought and received one anyway. One way to detect unauthorized users is to order your credit report and look through the list of inquiries for unfamiliar names or companies. (See above for information on how to order your credit report.) If someone has requested your report illegally, you may be able to sue for infringement of the Fair Credit Reporting Act — you may need the advocate's help to do so. You should also appeal to government agencies at the state and federal levels. The primary enforcer of the Federal Fair Credit Reporting Act is the Federal Trade Commission (FTC). (You can contact or file a complaint with the FTC at www.ftc.gov.) Apart from contacting the company to see if it agrees to address your complaint, the FTC may not handle your complaint individually, but if there are enough people complaining about the same company, it may investigate and take action to stop the company and perhaps get money back for the victims.

CHAPTER 6:

The Right Way to Check Your Credit Report

Checking your credit report on a regular basis is important — it not only can help to prevent errors that may cause you to be denied access to new credit but also can be helpful in uncovering whether or not you've been a victim of identity theft. And last but not least, since your credit score is based on the information contained within your credit reports, it's important to make sure that there are no errors on them that could lead to a lowered credit score.

Checking your credit reports can be a chore, but with the right information (which you'll have after reading this chapter), you'll see that getting your hands on your reports and checking them over is fast and easy!

Where to Obtain Your Credit Report

Go to www.AnnualCreditReport.com to get your credit report. This is the only website that is authorized by Federal law to provide you with the free credit report that the law entitles you to. While you will find many other websites that offer free credit reports, there are often strings attached.

How Often Are You Allowed a Free Copy of Your Credit Report?

By law, you are allowed to access your credit report for free once per year from each of the big three credit reporting agencies. You are also entitled to a free copy of your credit report if any of the following occur:

- You are unemployed but plan on looking for a job within 60 days.
- You're on welfare.
- Your report contains errors due to fraud (for example, identity theft).

Hot Tip: Avoid paying for pricey credit monitoring services by staggering your credit report requests instead. Ask for a report from Equifax in January, Experian in May, and TransUnion in September. For most people, this is a great way of monitoring your credit for free.

Remember: Although you are entitled to a free copy of your credit report periodically, you are not entitled to a free copy of your credit score — the credit reporting agencies, including FICO, are allowed to charge you for that.

Your 6-Step Credit Check Checklist

Now that you know where to get your credit report, here are the six steps to successfully checking it over.

1. Verify that your name, address, date of birth, and social security number are accurate.

Be on the lookout for name confusion. For example, Mike Smith or Michael Smith is likely ok, but Michael Smith II and Michael Smith I could be totally different people.

Ditto for Jr. and Sr. If either of these scenarios applies to you, be sure your credit report shows the correct title.

2. Read over the guide to interpreting a credit report that is provided by the credit bureau.

Credit reports often have codes that make no sense to a first-time user. Save yourself the frustration of reading their "foreign language" by reading through the user guide or help files that explain how to interpret the information and codes contained in your report.

I'll admit that it's dull and boring to read through the guide, but it'll be well worth it since it will save you tons of time when reading through your report. And besides, if you check your credit report regularly (and you should!), with time, the information contained in the guide will become committed to memory.

3. Look for any errors in account activity.

According to the US Government Accountability Office, 25% of all credit reports have errors, and about half of those errors are affecting the credit score. When you look over your credit reports, ensure that there isn't any incorrect information, such as claims that you paid late when you didn't.

Pay particular attention to any negative account activity, such as late or missed payments — if the information is accurate, so be it. But if the negative information is not correct, you can have it fixed.

4. Look for accounts that do not belong to you.

Make sure all of the accounts listed on your report actually belong to you. Sometimes, simple errors in Social Security numbers or misspelled names can lead to someone else's account information showing up on your report.

5. Check for duplicate accounts.

Sometimes, if an account is transferred from one company to another, due to a merger, for example, the account ends up on your credit report twice; once under each company name. This can lead to your amount of available credit being reported inaccurately.

6. Look for lines of credit that are inactive.

If you have lines of credit that are no longer needed, it may be worth closing them to "make room" for a new credit application somewhere else. However, I only recommend doing this if you need to since having unused credit can improve your credit score by helping to keep your credit utilization percentage lower.

The 2 Things You Must Do If You Find Errors on Your Credit Report

If you find any errors, here are the two steps that you must take to fix them. The error may be an innocent mistake or a sign of something more serious such as identity theft — either way, you need to find out and fix it.

1. In writing, inform the credit reporting agency that is showing an error on their report. Unless they consider your request frivolous, they are generally required to investigate within 30 days. To expedite the process, provide them with all the information (copies, not originals!) they could possibly need from you in order to begin their investigation.

2. In writing, inform the company that provided the inaccurate information to the credit reporting agency that they made an error and you are formally requesting an investigation. Provide

them with all relevant information in your possession that proves the accuracy of your claim. Again, send copies, not originals, of any documentation that you provide.

Expert Tip #1: Even if a credit reporting agency allows you to report an issue via telephone, this may not be your best option. Ideally, you ought to have copies of all correspondence so that you can refer to them if things get lost. Make photocopies of all written correspondence, save copies of any e-mails that you send, and take screenshots of any information you provide via online Contact Us forms.

To take a screenshot on a PC, press and hold the Alt button while you press the Print Screen key. The Print Screen key is located near the upper-right corner of your keyboard.

To take a screenshot on a Mac, press Command + Shift + 4 at the same time. Then drag the cursor to capture the portion of the screen that you wish to save a picture of.

Expert Tip #2: When mailing documentation, pay extra for the service that provides you with proof of delivery. This way, you'll be 100% certain that the information was received in a timely manner.

If you win your claim, the company that reported the inaccurate information must inform all three major credit bureaus of the error. In addition to that, the credit reporting agency whose report showed the error must provide you a corrected copy of your credit report for free.

Once the credit reporting agency agrees to correct the error, it could take a few weeks for the change to show up. If you require the correction to occur sooner in order to facilitate your approval for a loan, ask your lender about a rapid rescore. This service isn't available directly to consumers, but to lenders — it often allows for credit scores to be corrected within days.

So, say you're applying for a mortgage and correcting an error could lead to an increase in your score and a better interest rate for your mortgage. If you can provide your lender with proof of the error, they may be able to expedite a rapid rescore for you (extra fees may apply).

However, there are no guarantees that you'll be granted a rapid rescore, so the best option is to check over your credit reports a few months in advance and allow lots of time for any errors to be investigated and corrected.

5 Bonus Tips

1. If you are checking your credit report for the purposes of verifying accuracy before obtaining credit, be sure to ask the creditor which report and score system they use so you can check those first. You might as well start with the credit reports that are most important.

2. If you're like most people, checking each of your three credit reports once a year will be plenty to keep on top of things. As for your actual credit score, according to FICO, in a three-month period, 75% of people have a change in their credit score of less than 20 points — in other words, for most people, the month-to-month changes in their credit scores are relatively small. So, it's probably not worth paying for access to your credit score too often, unless you need to know your number to double-check what kind of shape you're in.

3. Generally speaking, collection accounts should be removed from your credit report after seven years — if you see any older than that, contact the relevant credit reporting agency and ask if it can be removed.

4. Don't worry if you see a bunch of "Account Management" or "Account Maintenance" inquiries from your credit card company — it is perfectly normal for them to check your credit

reports periodically, and these checks will not affect your credit score.

5. To check up on your FICO score, look at my FICO report — it will even tell you what negative factors might be affecting your score. You can order your score on their website: www.myfico.com

Summing Up

You've now learned how to get your hands on your credit report, how to check it over, and what to do if you find any mistakes.

Action Steps

1. Go to www.AnnualCreditReport.com and get your free credit report. Remember, unless there are extenuating circumstances, it's best to stagger your credit report orders so that you can check one every four months. For example, check Equifax in January, Experian in May, and TransUnion in September. However, if this is your first time checking your credit reports in a long time, it may be worthwhile to check them all at once this one time.

2. Go through the 6-step credit-check checklist and verify the accuracy of the information on your credit report.

3. If you find any errors, take action to correct them.

CHAPTER 7:

Ten Credit Score Myths to Unlearn

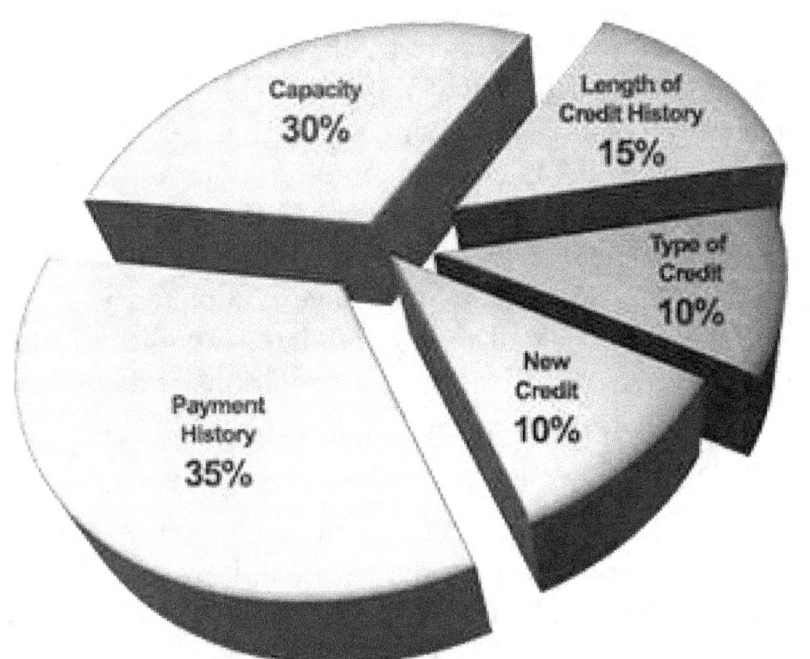

People are not always right. But they talk about everything, include credit scores. You have probably heard some damning information you do not know how real they could be. Your sixth sense keeps saying they are too good to be true. In other cases, you have probably heard it all, taken it all, and believe they are true, but that doesn't change it from being fallacies either.

Is there any way this book can help then? Definitely! Depending on whom you ask, there are various myths concerning Credit Scores, and here in this book, we will talk about the top 15 myths people pass around on Credit Scores. No matter what part of the country you stay in, you have likely heard most, if not all of these myths, and it is about time you changed how you view them.

1. 'I have a good credit score since I don't have a credit card debt': That is wrong! Your credit card is supposed to reveal your credit history, and you have credit history only when you have or have had debts. This is why it is not bad in any way to have debts in your credit report. Contrary to that perspective, it is possible to have debts in your credit report and still have excellent credit scores. Wondering why? It is because a credit score is not particular about whether you have loans at that moment or you don't. You may have completed your loan payments, but you paid at rather odd, late, and uncomfortable times that have violated the agreed regulations of the contract. In a case like that, you have paid up your debts, but you cannot have a great credit score.

Rather than that, a credit score would evaluate the debts you have taken up, how you honored the deal, how soon and how consistent you paid them up. That means that if you have debts, you are paying during the period your credit score is being computed, your debt will be evaluated according to the contract. It will look to find out when you started the contract, the agreed payment schedule, and how much you have played by the rules in the pact.

2. 'My credit score reduces every time someone calls for my credit report': This observation requires a careful approach. For one reason, your credit score indeed stands to be affected as a result of how often the credit report is requested. But it

doesn't affect your credit scores the way you assume it does. First, you should remember the four phases of a credit score. The personal section, the trade lines, judicial reports, and lastly, the section for the different individuals or firms who have recently requested your credit report. You will also remember that the last section of your credit record where those who requested for credit report recently are highlighted carries about 10%.

This means the number of people who have reviewed and within what period will have effects on your score. For example, you will likely get strong marks here if only two have recently reviewed your credit report in 3-6 months. In order cases, your scores reduce if more people have requested for it. This is to tell you that your credit score does not reduce every time someone calls for your credit card, but it will reduce when too many people have called for your card.

3. 'You should deliberately refuse to balance your credit card month by month-end': Many people heard that it is really bad of them to pay up all debts accumulated with their credit card by the month-end. Rather, they should extend the debts to the other months at one time or another. This way, at least, they can keep in touch with debts and build experience of lengthier and complicated debts, and not to worry, it won't affect their credit record in any way.

That seems quite awkward and hard to believe. Whether they are simple or complex loans is not even what matters, additional charges will be placed on your credit the moment you withdraw more than your credit limit in the month. That is not all, you will incur the last thing you want to have; poor credit scores. As far as the records prove, there is no known benefit of trying something like that, instead, everybody believes it has got negative impacts only. So, you need not try out theories and tales that could place you in financial difficulty. If you must experiment with something new, make sure it isn't this.

4. 'Your credit score cannot be easily spoilt': You will probably hear some boasting about how they are so sure your credit score can't get affected so easily. A lot of them think your credit reporting agencies would usually overlook the simple errors you make, the few debts you delayed, and the credit card charges you pended as long as you do not continue for a very long time. I find this very interesting. Having known for sure that these things are myths people try to picture in their heads so they could hold onto some hope when they make mistakes. They would usually boast about how they are sure little debts, little errors, and little recklessness can't do much harm. They often extend the duration of their loans. They don't feel the urgency to pay up their credit card charges as soon as they can too.

You honestly do not want to join that crew. Their ideas are simply unrealistic and preposterous. Credit Bureaus are charged to record every fact and figure, and they must put them all into consideration when grading your credit performance in the year. If you had had impressive records in these little records, would you want them overlooked?

5. 'If you have poor records, there's no way you can have a turnaround again': It is surprising to see that quite a lot of people believe this. They fear that there's no way anyone who has poor credits can have a turnaround. According to many, the poor records continue to linger in the records, and as such cannot be erased. Some others believe that it is always difficult to overwrite any bad record on a credit score. It drags down your grade and makes it extremely hard to make high scores,

always battling with the positive activities that could add to their grades.

But from an entirely different perspective, it is interesting to note that such policies are too bad to be true. They are unfound fallacies and stories that are not near accurate. Poor records are not permanent on your profile. The only reason they become permanent is if you repeat the same activities that got you bad grades from the start. For example, you got an auto loan from A&D Inc., agreed to pay up in six months, but extended the payment till about 10 months. You are bound to earn a low credit score with that, but if you perform better in other loans, your credit report will be gradually boosted.

6. 'You can't ever remove your bad records': This is one of the reasons many people feel they need to start again. It occurs a few times that you have a long and impressive credit history, but finances became harsh at some point and you couldn't go on with the payment policies on loans you have drawn earlier. You will likely earn poor grades with that, but when evaluated alongside your old records, you realize you still stand a chance. In some cases, these poor records go on for a long while that they fill your profile and you doubt whether you can ever wriggle out of them.

For some, they have more than enough poor records of payment on their profile, and at some point, they began to keep up with things. They earned more and they paid their loans better, but their new records are always downed by their old records. In either case, you will likely feel tempted to open a new credit account. Particularly if you believe the poor records will always lurk in your profile. Many people jettison their venerated profiles and take on new ones, therefore, finding it very challenging to secure the trust of new credit companies.

In most cases, you do not have to do that. Whether you make further credits or not, whether you have impressive records afterward or not, the United States Fair Act mandates that after seven years, you can remove a poor record from your profile permanently, which means it will no longer be considered or referenced in your credit card or credit score.

7. 'There is just a credit score for you': This assumption is usually made by people who are just arriving into the credit arena, and perhaps, of course, some older ones paying little attention. They assume that only one credit score is for them in many instances, and therefore, do not see the need to pursue others. They believe what you get from TransUnion will likely be the result from Experian and so forth. They also believe that the same grading method is used. In truth, there are different models and different credit reporting agencies. If they work exactly, then there really may not be the need to have more than one. As a practical example, it is possible to be graded 780 of 1000 if graded by Experian, and you get 830 when graded by TransUnion. You can then decide who forwards to your crediting company or what you send to them if they are accustomed to a particular company.

So, starting with your Credit Bureaus, be sure that you will always get different results from different organizations. Besides that, there are various models used in grading your credit scores too. FICO is the most used, and definitely what you are familiar with, but there are a couple of others like Credit Xpert, CE credit score, TransRisk, Vantage, and so many others. While they are fairly similar, each of them works in a unique style and you would get different scores from each of them, which may in spite of that, be in a range.

8. 'Employers consider credit scores in employment': Because many companies request the credit report of their applicants,

many believe they use the credit scores generated in the credit report to evaluate their potential employers and, sometimes, grade how responsible they would be at work. Financial crossroads reports that many even assume the sole reason employers request credit report is to review how much their applicants have been in debt and could at any time abscond with the company's finances.

These are all absurd claims that have been on the street for such a long time, but tales like this must not get into your head. You simply can't afford to believe them. You can relate to this by considering yourself the Employer, would you turn down an impressive application simply because the applicant is in debt? Don't we get work to clear our bills and live comfortably? It is how everyone lives.

Most employers only request credit reports because they would like to confirm the basic data about you. Are you an existing, active member of the community? They have an idea how much you need the job too while confirming your facts on your finances, and that's all there is to it.

9. 'Having a lot of money in the bank boosts your credit score': Another myth going on in the minds of people about credit scores is about bank accounts. Many feel that once they have some huge cash in their account, it can be rated alongside their credit scores, and in some way, they should get much better grading. Without even being asked, many would attach their bank details or tax information to their credit reports when presenting it themselves. To some, having enough in your bank means you really have been finding your way off incurring debts. So, you have avoided using credits and you should be awarded pretty high credit high scores. But that's not near the case; your credit score is your credit score. It is not your financial score. It is meant to supply information on your

credit, not your finances as a whole, so having a large bank account says nothing about getting very high scores. Do you want high scores? Play by the rules, there's no two-way.

10. 'Paying off an old debt saves your credit score': Humans are especially intelligent beings. Some way, they are sure that they can always bend a few rules and get exactly what they want. It is the reason they would believe that a few days to when their credit report would be submitted, they could pay up old and overdue debts on their file and get the high scores they deserve from the start. Many often forget that the scores are not calculated by finding out whether the debt is fully cleared or not, rather by measuring how much the policies are obeyed.

Here's what I am reiterating. You got an auto loan in January 2109 with a six-month regulation, which means you should pay up the funds by July 2019. Due to errors solely on your part, you could not pay up the funds at that moment. You still have some amount of the loan left to be paid when in November 2019, you desire to take up a mortgage loan with another firm. Contrary to popular belief, paying such loans at that moment does not rid you of a bad credit score, as your credit score is projected to display how you played by the agreed regulations within the deadline, not exactly whether you paid up or not. So, if you are assuming paying at such moments can save you in some way, take your mind off it all.

CHAPTER 8:

What's a Good Credit Score?

In the current economy, it's a lot harder to qualify for a loan. Presently, you need an excellent credit score to qualify for most types of credit. So, what's a good credit score rating?

850 is immaculate credit and the most elevated credit score rating conceivable; however, I've never personally observed anybody with an 850. A good credit score begins in the 670 territory. Scores lower than 670 are not viewed as good credit.

Understanding FICO Credit Score

FICO Scores are one of numerous elements almost all lenders in the U.S. think about when they settle on key credit choices. Truth be told, a US News and World Report article expressed that "The FICO Score is the No. 1 bit of information to decide the amount you'll pay on a loan and whether you'll get credit." Such choices incorporate whether to endorse your credit application, what credit terms to offer you, and whether to expand your credit limit once your credit account is built up. FICO Scores are utilized by a huge number of creditors, including the 50 biggest lenders, making it the most generally utilized credit score. At the point when you acknowledge new credit and oversee it tenaciously by reliably paying as agreed, you show to lenders that you speak to a good credit hazard. Lenders utilize your credit history as a method for assessing how well you have dealt with your credit to date.

A FICO Score is a three-digit number determined from the credit information on your credit report at a customer reporting agency (CRA) at a specific point in time. It outlines information in your credit report into a solitary number that lenders can use to survey your credit chance rapidly, reliably, unbiasedly, and fairly. Lenders utilize your FICO Scores to assess your credit hazard — that you are so prone to pay your credit commitments as agreed. Also, it causes you to obtain credit dependent on your genuine acquiring and repayment history without thought of disallowed types of information, for example, race or religion. Your FICO Scores from every agency might be diverse on the grounds that FICO Scores depend exclusively on the particular credit information in that agency's credit file, and not all lenders report to each of the three CRAs. Indeed, even in occurrences where the lender reports to each of the three CRAs, the planning of when information from credit grantors is refreshed to your credit file may make contrasts in your score over the three CRAs.

Notwithstanding the three-digit number, a FICO Score incorporates "score factors" which are the top factors that affected the score. Tending to a few of these score variables can assist you with improving your monetary wellbeing after some time. Having a good FICO Score can place you in a superior situation to qualify for credit or better terms later on.

FICO Scores are utilized by lenders regarding a wide assortment of credit Items such as:

- Credit Cards
- Auto Loans
- Personal Loans & Lines of Credit
- Student Loans
- Home Equity Lines & Loans
- Mortgages

How FICO Scores Help You

A FICO Score gives lenders a quick, objective, and predictable gauge of your credit risk. Prior to the utilization of scoring, the credit allowing procedure could be moderate, conflicting, and unjustifiably one-sided. Here are a few different ways FICO Scores help you.

Get credit quicker

FICO Scores can be conveyed immediately, helping lenders accelerate credit card and loan endorsements. This implies when you apply for credit, you'll find a solution all the more immediately, even inside seconds. Indeed, even a home loan application can be endorsed a lot quicker for borrowers who score over the lender's base score necessity. FICO Scores likewise permit retail locations, web locales, and different lenders to make "moment credit" decisions. Remember that FICO Scores are just one of the numerous factors lenders think about when settling on a credit decision.

Credit decisions are more attractive

Utilizing FICO Scores, lenders can concentrate on the realities identified with credit risk instead of their genuine beliefs or inclinations. Factors, for example, your sexual orientation, race, religion, nationality, and conjugal status are not considered by FICO Scores. So, when a lender utilizes your FICO Score, it is getting an assessment of your credit history that is reasonable and objective.

More established credit issues mean less

In the event that you have had issues covering tabs previously, it won't frequent you everlastingly (except if you keep on taking care of tabs late). The effect of past credit issues on your FICO Scores blurs over the long haul and as ongoing great installment designs appear on your credit report.

A Higher FICO Score sets you aside cash

At the point when you apply for credit — regardless of whether it's a credit card, a vehicle loan, an individual loan, or a home loan — lenders need to see how risky you are as a borrower so as to settle on a decent decision. Your FICO Scores may influence not just a lender's decision to concede you a credit, yet in addition, how much credit and on what terms (interest rate, for instance). Remember that FICO Scores are just one of the numerous factors lenders think about when settling on a credit decision.

A higher FICO Score can assist you with fitting the bill for better rates from lenders — most times, the higher your score, the lower your interest rate and installments. The contrast between a FICO® Score of 620 and 760, for instance, can be a huge number of dollars over the life of a loan.

Think about these two models:

Two unique individuals are getting $230,000 on a 30-year contract. A borrower that has a FICO Score of 760 could pay $211 less every month in interest in contrast to a borrower with a FICO Score of 630. That is an investment fund of $75,960 over the life of the loan.

On a $20,000, 48-month automobile loan, the borrower with a FICO Score of 720 could pay $131 less every month in interest as compared to a borrower with a FICO Score of 580. That is a reserve fund of $6,288 over the life of the loan.

How to Obtain a Good Credit Score

There are five criteria that your credit is scored upon which are rather simple to follow.

1. The Payment History accounts for 35% of your credit score.

Do you pay your bills on time? If you don't do anything else yet make timely payments, you will have a good credit score in two years. Clearly, staying away from new assortments, court activities, and most effectively, late pays will support your credit. Past wrongdoing assumes the biggest job in harming your credit score. One ongoing multi-day late payment will bring down your credit score, in all probability by 20! A few late payments and your score will drop extremely far, exceptionally fast. Multi-day lates hurt your score considerably more, and multi-day lates are the main problem. Know that the later the wrongdoing, the more negative the impact on your score. One multi-day late a month ago will sting more than even a multi-day late 4-5 years prior (5-10). Make sure to remain over your debt. Take alert to make timely payments and deal with accounts before they are late or go to assortment. Try not to overextend yourself so that it harms your odds of making timely payments. If that you have old late pays that can't be questioned off your credit report, realize that time heals old injuries and your score will increase given that no new misconducts are reported. Pay before the Grace Period placed on your Credit Cards. Creditors charge extra expenses for late payments. This is an exceptionally enormous benefit place for a bank. Presently, not exclusively is there due date. However, there is likewise a due time. A bank may charge a $30–$35 expense for being 2 hours late on your payments! (Be sure to look at the fine print, all things considered.) Also, numerous banks have actualized under multi-day effortlessness periods, abbreviated from 30 days, to increase overdue charges. Try not to sit tight for the due date! Get your payments in fast or pursue automatic charge payments on the web.

2. Amount Owed accounts for 30% of your credit score.

The credit scoring model determines credit balance, usually against your high credit limit. This is calculated in rates. It's imperative to keep your balances as low as could be allowed. In the event that you have a card with a $5,000 credit limit, keeping your balance beneath $500 places you in the 10% scope of accessible credit. There are thresholds in debt proportion that will make your credit score bounce higher. These thresholds are 70%, half, 30%, and 10%. If you can't pay off your credit cards the whole distance, pay them down BELOW the following conceivable edge. Calculate your credit limits along these lines. In the event that you have a card with a $5,000 limit, increase 5000 x.10 (or.30,.50,.70). You will need to pay your balance underneath these sums. For this situation — under $500 (or $1500, $2500, or $3500). Keep in mind; the principal activity is to check your credit report for credit limits. If that your high limit isn't reporting, the scoring model will utilize your balance as your credit limit. This implies you're utilizing 100% of your availability. Call your creditor and make sure they right it. Conveyance of debt is a simple method to make sure you keep up a solid score. Attempt to have a good spread of debt with a lower balance to limit proportion. For instance, it's better to possess $2,000 on 5 cards than it is to possess $10,000 on a card with others paid off. In case you're knocking up towards your credit limits, apply for more credit, or request an increase in credit from your current accounts. This criterion depends on all-out availability, not an estimate of availability. It doesn't make a difference if you acquire $500 or $50,000. It's the means by which you handle it that matters. Disseminating debt onto extra cards or credit lines can assist you with raising your score rapidly.

3. The Length of Credit History counts for 15% of your credit score.

Length of credit history implies to what extent you've had your credit accounts. If you've had a record for 15 years, it is more grounded than having another record open for just two months. An important hint here is to never close your credit cards. Keep your old accounts open in the event that they are in good standing, regardless of whether you don't utilize them and there's a zero balance. Keep in mind, however, you do need to utilize your credit lines something like clockwork. Accounts unused for 6 months become idle and are overlooked by the credit bureaus, except if there is a reprobate action joined to that record. Keeping your credit lines open likewise helps in improving your credit availability, clarified in the past segment.

If looking to include credit, ask your card organization to increase your credit limit. The best spot to increase your credit lines, besides getting another card, is to broaden your line on an old record with a good long history. Be sure they report the credit amount increment to the bureaus accurately. A normal factor of amazingly good credit scores is long credit narratives. Credit reports that possess old accounts with a fifteen to twenty-year history are probably going to have a lot higher scores. It is, nonetheless, conceivable to add old tradelines to your credit report.

4. Amount of New Credit accounts for 10% of your credit score

A new credit implies fresh out-of-the-box new accounts as of late open. You do need to begin someplace, yet construct gradually. In the event that you have recently applied for 10 credit cards, banks will, in general, accept the likelihood that possibly you've lost your employment and are needing a backup plan. Attempt to begin with one little credit extension and work from that point. Make sure that you can deal with the payments reliably, being rarely late, and keep your balances as low as could be allowed, or totally paid off.

5. Kind of Credit utilized accounts for 10% of your credit score.

The credit scoring model loves to see that you have an assortment of types of credit in your file. The absolute best arrangement of credit is to have a loan on a home, a vehicle payment, and a couple of credit cards. This credit is spread crosswise over various types of lenders and the sort of credit reached out to you. There are a couple of types of credit to avoid. Payday loans are terrible spots to have credit with, and your scores endure a shot for having these types of high-risk loans. Other very awful types of credit are the offers that enable you to have no payments for a year. These are hazardous on the grounds that the conditions of the understanding may incorporate that in the event that you don't pay the loan off in a year, on day 366 you will owe the whole year's worth of payments at normally 20% interest. This is a debacle already in the works. Individuals who more than once go for these offers are individuals who fall into credit difficulty. You ought not to have that sort of credit on your credit report.

There are a few things to consider when one is contemplating what is a good credit score. One method for evaluating the capacity of a borrower to pay back a loan is to see that person's credit score. The scores can be high or low or in the center. In the event that a score is high, at that point, it is accepted that a person would have the option to obtain significant credit and can without much of a stretch pay back assets loaned to them. If a score is low, the recognition is the inverse. A low score will make lenders careful, and it won't be simple for one to have monies stretched out to them. In a lender's eyes, different scores may mean various things, contingent upon the sort of scoring framework that specific creditor employments. This important credit score one obtains is useful to those choosing whether or not to loan reserves. Those substances expanding credit can make sense of the amount of cash to offer an individual and with what interest rate also.

Credit scores are made out of a varying level of numbers, somewhere in the range of 300-850. A score is made up of a range of appropriate factors. A gander at the payment history information comprises 35% of the score. Watching the amount a person owes is 30%. The credit history life span is 15% of the score. New spending information creates 10%. Thought of the different sorts of credit utilized is staying 10% of the score number.

Equifax, Experian, and TransUnion are three credit reporting offices. One free yearly credit report can be obtained from every one of these organizations for an absolute check of three reports per year. It is important to process the substance that is on one's report with extreme attention to detail. Information that isn't accurate and right can sometimes be found. Sometimes, errors in late payment content, payment chronicles, and amounts of money owed can be seen. A person can be sure in looking into the report that there is no wholesale fraud also.

Tips for raising your FICO scores

In the event that your Classic FICO scores are in the pits, don't surrender. You can accomplish a few things to raise them; for example, the accompanying:

- Regularly audit every one of your credit files for errors, fragmented information, and outdated information; all of which can lower your credit scores. In the event that you find any of these issues, get them adjusted as quickly as could be allowed.
    • Stay alert for signs that your personality has been taken. If a character criminal opens new credit accounts in your name, defaults on the accounts, or runs up your current accounts, your credit scores will be harmed.

- Pay your debts on time. On-time payments are the most ideal approach to improve your Classic FICO scores. The more drawn out your history of on-time payments, the better; so in case you're behind on any of your accounts, get made up for a lost time as quickly as possible.

- Pay down the exceptional credit balances you can find on your credit cards. The more you get closer to your credit limits as your balance increases, the more harm you're doing to your credit scores. Additionally, accelerate the rate at which you pay off installment loans; for example, vehicle loans.

- Don't manage high credit card balances by moving the debt starting with one credit card, then onto the next so as to exploit lower interest rates. Rather, center on paying off those debts.
- Only apply for credit that you only need. Indeed, even one application for new credit will lower your Classic FICO to some degree.
- Don't close old accounts, regardless of whether you never use them, and they have zero balances. The Classic FICO scoring model considers to what extent you've had credit. Indeed, having many credit accounts harms your scores; however, once you have them, your scores have just endured a shot.

CHAPTER 9:

How to Use and Fix Identity Theft

CATEGORY	SCORE
Excellent (30% of People)	750 - 850
Good (13% of People)	700 - 749
Fair (18% of People)	650 - 699
Poor (34% of People)	550 - 649
BAD (16% of People)	350 - 549

Did you ever wonder if people are becoming the perpetrators of identity theft? Or maybe you have been and you're not sure how it happened. There are plenty of approaches used by hackers to get your personal information ahold.

In this chapter, we'll explore what identity theft is, how to protect your identity, common identity theft ways, where to turn, and what to do if you're a victim of identity theft, plus how to rebound if it happens to you.

Theft of identity is one form of fraud. It is defined as taking or claiming the identity of another person to use existing accounts, open new credit accounts, or receive other benefits for a fraudulent reason from their personal information. A person's credit cards are usually used for making purchases. Social Security cards and numbers were also taken to establish new credit in your name.

How Identity Theft Happens

Identity theft happens in a variety of ways; hackers obtain access to your personal information by removing it from your purse or wallet, impersonating an official representative, and accessing your identity through mail and computer technology. Here are some of the ways identity thieves get your personal data:

- Skimming. Occasionally, there may be a special storage device connected to the card reader while you swipe your credit card or debit card during a normal transaction. This system collects and stores up to several hundred numbers per credit card at a time. When you transfer the details to a computer, the identity thief will have access to your information without even realizing it.

- Hacking. Most identity thieves are also hackers. For businesses that have personal records for the place, they will use smart technology to hack into your personal computers or computer systems. Many banks were also victims of malware and all of their clients may have been victims of identity theft.

- Stealing mail. The e-mail provides credit card statements, tax information, bank statements, credit deals pre-approved, and even new checks. Thieves will rob from your mailbox right away and were even known to have mail sent to them. This confidential information is at their disposal and can help them rob your identity.

- Dumpster diving. Identity thieves also rummage through your personal garbage, something that often occurs in companies. Robbers search and locate bank account numbers, credit card numbers, financial statements, and other personal information through the trash.

- Stealing purses and wallets. Often, identity thieves rummage through your personal trash, something that sometimes occurs in companies. Thieves dig through the garbage and find bank account numbers, credit card numbers, financial statements, and other personal data.

- Employees of businesses. Identity thieves can sometimes steal personal records from businesses. This could be an employee's role-taking company documents from his or her own boss in order to gain access to confidential information. Many identity thieves at a business may conspire with an employee who can give them access to personal records. Therefore, workers receiving credit reports can violate their rights to that information.

- E-mails and phone calls. Identity hackers were known to impersonate your broker, trustee, or another company representative by calling or giving you an e-mail. Do not do so if you receive a mysterious phone call or e-mail demanding your personal information to either check your account or to claim some money. They most likely try to steal your credit card number, Social Security number, or other account numbers, whatever the scheme.

- Home theft. Many robbers are trying to break into your home not to steal your Television or jewels, but to take your name. They will steal tax information, bank account numbers, Social Security numbers, number of credit card accounts, and any other personal information they might discover.

What to Do If You Are a Victim of Identity Theft

Have you ever seen this happen? You just received a collection notice in the mail for an account you didn't use or even know about, you received a credit card in the mail you never wanted or opened, or you were simply turned down for a loan or credit card due to a low FICO score with accounts that weren't even yours. If there has been one of these cases, you are most likely a victim of identity theft.

You might feel robbed, betrayed, and left wondering how this might happen to you. Your credit scores were most likely impacted negatively. You may need a loan or credit, and this condition prohibits you from receiving it. To fix the damage that has already happened and to mitigate potential future harm, you need to take control and figure out what to do next.

Criminal laws regulate identity theft. According to the Identity Theft and Assumption Deterrence Act of 1998 (3. 18 U.S.C. subsection 1028(a) (7)), it is a felony to "consciously pass or use, without legal authority, a means of identifying another person with the intention of committing, or aiding or abetting, any criminal conduct that constitutes a breach of Federal law or that constitutes a crime under any State or local statute applicable." The law is in place to provide offenders with a consolidated complaint process, as well as improve the criminal laws surrounding identity theft. If you're a victim of identity theft, prompt action is required. The law allows claimants to challenge unauthorized charges; however, there are some time limits that need to be followed.

- Notify the creditor. When you find unauthorized charges on your credit or debit card, then you were most likely a victim of identity theft. The good news is that the Equal Credit Billing Act limits any responsibility for unauthorized charges to $50. When you discover the unauthorized charges, you will have to write down your trustee, disputing the questionable payments.

    Write the letter of disagreement to the agency "Billing inquiries" of your creditor. Make sure you send the certified letter to your trustee and you know it's hitting you. Notify the creditor as soon as the unwanted payment is identified and make sure that your letter hits them within 60 days of the first bill revealing the mistake. Keep yourself a copy of the letter. Under the statute, the creditor must respond within 30 days of receiving the message, and the conflict must be settled within two billing cycles.

- Notify your bank. If your debit card has been stolen, you will report it to your bank within two working days. Under the Electronic Fund Transfer Act, you will only be held liable for $50 in unauthorized charges; however, you will be responsible for $500 of unauthorized charges if you report the unauthorized charges between three and 60 days. Unless you wait until 60 days later, you can lose all of the money stolen from your account. If your debit card has a Visa or MasterCard mark, both firms will limit your liabilities to $50 per card in unauthorized charges.

It's better that you alert your suppliers and banks as soon as you can or your debit cards, credit cards, and even personal checks have been stolen if you detect fraudulent charges. The longer you wait to contact the lender, the greater the chance that some or all of the unauthorized charges will be placed on you.

- Fraud alert. If you've been a victim of identity theft, it's important to create a warning about fraud. If you call credit reporting agencies, you will have to choose between two different types of fraud alerts — the expanded warning and the original notice.

The expanded notice entitles you to receive two free credit reports from each credit reporting agency per year; however, for seven years, the fraud alert must stay on your register. The most common type of warning against fraud is the original alarm. This will stay 90 days on your file and will send you one free credit report from each of the three reporting agencies.

You have to have a police report and evidence of the theft or attempted fraud to create an extended warning. You may request that for your protection, only the last four digits of your Social Security number appear on your credit report. You may also cancel any warning about fraud at any time.

To set up a fraud alert for your own protection is in your best interest. Creditors will take more precautions when reviewing your credit or loan application and you will be alerted if someone uses your identity to attempt to open accounts. This means the robber can't open credit in your name. You will notify the other credit reporting offices whether you call one of the credit reporting agencies to set up the fraud alert.

Your credit report and credit score are important to you and to your future earnings. Make sure you check them regularly to ensure you're not a victim of identity theft.

- Police report. If you suspect that you are a victim of identity theft, it is in your best interests to lodge a police report. Some creditors may require that a police report be used as evidence of the incident. Many police stations hesitate to take a call on identity theft. Assure your submission is permanent. Make sure that you have a copy of the report for your history because credit card companies and banks may need to see the report and search for unauthorized charges. Remember, make sure that you have the name and phone number of the prosecutor in case the investors need to talk to him or her.

- Social Security Administration. If your Social Security card has been stolen, or you know your Social Security number has been used to open new accounts, you will call the Department of Social Security. They will, most of the time, issue you a new Social Security number and card. To apply for a new Social Security number, you must provide evidence that someone using your account is still harming you. Your sex, U.S. residency or legal immigration status, and name will need to be confirmed.

- Postal inspector. When you believe that your mail was robbed or sent to a different location, you were most likely a victim of identity theft in which a criminal rummaged through your mail or used a Change of

Address form to give them your mail. Contact the postal inspector for documentation, and prosecute this fraud.

- Department of Motor Vehicles. If you have been stolen your driver's license, you need to contact the state agency that issued your license. Most of the time, you can locate their contact information by checking the Department of Motor Vehicles in your state online. They will cancel your license and give you instructions on how to get another license.

- Federal Trade Commission. You will report the crime to the Federal Trade Commission (FTC) if you've been a victim of identity theft. Call them at IDTHEFT (877) or at www.idtheft.gov. Although the FTC does not prosecute identity theft, it exchanges concerns with local regulatory bodies that support the federal fight against identity theft.

Protecting Yourself from Identity Theft

To deter identity theft from happening to you, it's important that you immediately start taking proactive steps. Additionally, if you've been a victim of identity theft, it's crucial that you deal quickly with the aftermath to prevent any further harm.

Here are a few of the preventive steps you can take to stop becoming an identity theft victim:

- Check your mailbox. You will search the mailbox regularly so that there is no mail left in there for longer than a day or overnight. If your mailbox doesn't have a security feature, you should consider getting a lock for your mailbox. Sometimes, consider holding the mail at the post office when you go on vacation so you don't become a victim of identity theft.

- Secure your computer. Hackers use smart programming to get what they want from your computer; however, if you are making your computer secure, you can stop them from accessing your private information. Do not store in your hard drive financial information, and make sure that your firewall protects your computer. Wireless routers also allow you to create a single password. Make sure you create a password that contains a combination of numbers, characters, and letters. Don't put your passwords on your Mac.

- Use a locked file cabinet. Ensure that your financial documents, social security cards, passports, bank statements, credit card statements, and tax information are stored in a locked cabinet or secured safe.

- Keeping a list of all your credit cards and account numbers in this secured safe or closed filing cabinet is a good idea. That way, you will have a complete list of account numbers, suppliers, and contact information to dial in an emergency if your wallet or purse ever gets stolen. Do not leave this document outside a locked/secure location anywhere else. Don't put your Social Security card in your wallet or purse, either. Hold that also in your safe.

- Shred important documents. Do not dispose of your bank accounts, credit card statements, or other financial documents. Thieves have been known to search through the garbage of people seeking personal information that they might use to rob their identity. Instead of throwing away all your important personal records, cover yourself by shredding them. Do not also cut out pre-approved credit card offers, but rip them.

- Check credit reports. Checking your credit reports once a year is a wise idea. Under the Equal and Accurate Credit Transactions Act, the three credit reporting agencies can provide you with one free credit report each year.

CHAPTER 10:

The Right Mindset

Many folks suffer a financial crisis at some point. They may have to deal with overspending, loss of a job, and a family member or personal illness. These financial problems can be, and usually are, overwhelming. To make these situations worse, most people don't even know where to begin to solve these financial dilemmas. Our goal here is to shine some light on the strategies to help get youth. Accumulating basic consumer debt will chain you into slavery and you could possibly spend your life held down by your own obligations to repay these loans. Who do you work for? I don't care what you say; the real answer is your creditors if you are currently stuck paying debts. There are many forms of "dumb debt" you can get trapped into. We are all sold images and lifestyles hundreds of times per day to provoke this materialistic behavior.

The person or institution lending you the money is trusting that you have the ability to hold up your end of the bargain, basically. Sometimes, it may seem impossible to live your life without the option to get credit, but this is what bad credit eventually leads to. Since your ability to repay a loan has been affected, either by the inability to pay or a series of misunderstandings, other lenders will become skeptical when it comes to granting you new credit.

But how do you get credit in the first place? What is the process you have to go through to loan money? Well, it all starts with a credit application to a bank or some other party that has the necessary finances. Your application is reviewed and, if they think there won't be a problem with getting their money back, you sign a contract and get your money in no time. This application contains a large amount of relevant information about yourself such as your employment situation, your monthly income, and other credits or obligations like rent, for instance. The application you submit to a lender is used to obtain a credit report from one or several reporting agencies, depending on how much money you need. These two documents are given scores and, if your score is enough, you'll get the money you need. If not, your application will be rejected. If you don't fall into any of these categories, then a judgment call has to be made by the person or institution providing the credit. The more "good credit" criteria you meet, the more likely it is that you will get your credit.

However, there are several things that you must consider before you put yourself into the category of citizens unaffected by bad credit. First of all, the lenders look for certain things in your application, such as an up-to-date credit report and no late payments on your other financial obligations. They are interested to see if you've had a job for more than a year and have a stable income, as well as a stable residence. They also evaluate the situation of your utility and phone bills, and appreciate it if you include information about additional credit cards or other types of cards. It is not only banks and money lenders that look at this type of information. Sometimes, if you want to get a new job, your employer will conduct this type of research too, so maintaining good credit is crucial in these troubled times we live in.

What type of credit should you get? That depends on what you plan to do with the money. The most used types of credit are secured and signature credits. For smaller loans, there's no need for that as no institution would like to end up with a store of household items, so they lend you money or issue a credit card in your name simply based on the strength of your credit so far.

There is hope; you, as the borrower, have many options to get rid of debt. You can take advantage of budgeting and other techniques, such as debt consolidation, debt settlement, credit counseling, and bankruptcy procedures. You just have to choose the best strategy that will work for you. When choosing from the various options, you have to consider your debt level, your discipline, and plans for the future.

The Good Debt

Some people find it hard to live debt-free, at least they will have some debt to pay off. While some debts are discouraged, good debt is considered as the money you borrow so that you can pay for things that you really need or things that increase in value. On the flip side, bad debt is one that arises from things that you only want and often decreases in value.

Of course, debt isn't a bad thing; it's just how you use the money that matters.

For a good debt, you will always have a good reason to justify it, and a developed plan for paying it so that you can clear the debt as quickly as possible.

An individual with good debt will also have the cheapest methods of borrowing money. They will do this by looking at the borrowing method, rate of interest, credit amount, and charges that are appropriate to them.

Sometimes, it may imply a deal with the least possible interest rate, but sometimes, it may not.

Examples of good debt

1. Paying for medical care. There is no fixed amount of money to borrow to ensure your loved one stays healthy. You can manage to pay off the money you borrow, but it is impossible to replace a human life. If a person requires expensive treatments to ensure they remain healthy, this would be an acceptable debt, no matter what.

2. Borrow money for education. When you apply for a student loan debt, you aren't making the wrong decision. In general, people with college degrees earn more income in their life than those without a degree.

    And applying for a student loan so that you can support the education of your child defeats the idea of using your savings. After all, you cannot borrow money to pay for your savings. Multiple government programs provide low-interest student loans, and you can always cut student loan interest on your taxes.

3. Taking out a mortgage on a home. Taking a loan of this amount can be overwhelming, but purchasing a house creates ownership in something that will house you and generate some retirement money. Even while you struggle to clear your debt, you may consider it an advantage to put any available liquid cash as a deposit, though it may not be the right choice.

   A home mortgage interest is cut on your taxes, and the rate of interest is lower on your home loan than on the credit card. In other words, it is important to have money to pay for other expenses instead of credit.

   Though purchasing a house was initially considered a strong, future-proof investment, certain homeowners do find themselves on the wrong side on their home mortgage loan. They owe banks more than the value of their homes. However, strategic planning, purchasing only what you can afford, and maintaining low interest by having good credit may allow you to purchase a home that one day you will own completely.

4. Buying a car. If you don't have public transport in your area, or you cannot manage to get someone with whom you can carpool, then you may have to consider buying a car. An auto loan can either be "good" or "bad," but the main thing is to ensure that the auto loan is good debt, so look for the lowest possible rates on your loan. In addition, you need to make a large down payment while ensuring that you remain with some cash on hand just in case you need it.

Your best goal should be to go for a used car model instead of a brand-new one, possibly saving yourself thousands on the sticker price and the interest that is paid throughout the loan.

5. Business loans. While this may not be seen as good debt, borrowing money to begin a business or expand a business is perhaps a great idea if the business is thriving. After all, you need money to make more money, right?

Sometimes, you may have to borrow capital to employ new people, purchase a new device, pay for advertisement, or even develop the first new widget you designed. The point is that you borrow this money to expand the business or increase income, then this will count as good debt.

What is Bad Debt?

Bad debt is that which depletes your wealth and isn't affordable. Plus, it provides no means to pay for itself.

Bad debts may have no realistic repayment plans and usually deplete when people buy things on impulse. If you aren't sure whether you can repay the money, then don't borrow the money because that will be a bad debt.

Examples of bad debt

1. The credit card debt. A typical household in the United States has a balance of more than $10,000 on their credit card every month. However, the debt usually increases faster than we may realize and is always used to purchase things that we want instead of need. It is easier to think that you can afford something using a card than paying it with cash.

2. Borrowing from a 401K. When you ask for money from a 401K program, you will need to chat with the IRS, and if you aren't using the money to purchase a home, you will need to pay the loan in five years. If you fail to pay it back, you risk being charged with a severe penalty. Also, the interest that you pay on the loan will get taxed twice.

   You can't get a loan to fund your retirement. For that reason, borrowing money from your retirement plan to use it to pay for anything that isn't part of retirement is a bad idea. You will be putting your retirement at risk when you get a loan from a 401k, so don't make this mistake.

3. Payday loans. It may appear easy to borrow money from payday loan firms, but it is hard to pay it back. These companies offer loans with very high interest rates. The companies take advantage of the fact that many people need that money. As a result, borrowing a small amount may end up costing you a lot.

   Payday loans aren't considered the worst kind of debt that you can take on. If you really need a short-term loan, it is better to go for a cash advance on a credit card rather than borrow money from these firms.

Using Consolidation or Settlement Strategies to Pay Down Debts

Debt consolidation is another strategy that can be used to manage your debts. It involves combining two or more debts at a lower interest rate that you are currently at.

But, it is worth doing your research and making some phone calls to see if there is a company that's willing to work with you.

If you can lower your monthly bill to a manageable level, at an interest rate that's reasonable, that can make all the difference in handling your debt.

Like many strategies, you have had the option of settling your debts with companies for decades. Lenders always want as much money as you can give them versus being shafted for the entire amount in a bankruptcy. It is just that consolidation and settlement options rose in popularity during the recent financial crisis, making it appear in more articles and news pieces than ever before.

If you have savings to pay off your debts, then start with the most expensive. Otherwise, utilize settlement options where you are able to reduce the amount owed if you pay a certain amount right now. As long as the account shows paid in full, with strong payment history, your scores are going to increase. It doesn't matter if you needed to use debt settlement strategies to make the debt end. It just matters that you have paid the debt off instead of letting it go into arrears.

Negotiate with Credit Companies

Another thing not a lot of people know is that you can negotiate with credit companies. So, you're able to take the collection letter they send you or a past due notice that has been sent to you and discuss it with them. In many cases, they will take a lower amount than what's on the bill just so that they can guarantee they'll get something

Let's say you owe Discover $1,000. They really want to get their money, so they send you a past due notice. But for several months you've ignored that past due notice, and now they've sent it to collections. The collections agency may offer you a settlement. Maybe they say they'll take $900 if you just pay it to them right then and there. You have the opportunity to call them and request that they take a lesser amount.

If you talk to the collection agency and they agree to take a lesser amount, you will have to send that payment in full. Make sure that when you send them the check, you write out the words 'paid in full' on the check. Make a copy of the check for your own records as well. Once they cash that check, your account is legally considered to be paid in full and they are no longer able to come after you for more money.

Cut the Credit Cards

If you're looking to save some money, then you need to make sure you're spending less. That means getting rid of all those credit cards. If you're able to avoid the temptation to purchase things, you can put one credit card in the back of your purse or wallet. Choose a card that will work anywhere such as a major credit card company. This is for emergencies only. An emergency doesn't mean you found something that you really want to have. It means that your car broke down and needs to be towed, or you run out of gas. The rest of the credit cards you decide to keep should be locked up somewhere in your home. Put them in a safe or lockbox. This way you have to actively think about getting the card out again before you're able to actually use it. This will keep you from using the card in a spur of the moment fashion and will ensure that you still have it available if absolutely necessary. The best thing to do is make one to two small purchases on your credit card every few months. Try to space out using different cards so that none of them get taken but you don't owe very much money each month. You want to keep the amount negligible. That means it is low enough that it really doesn't affect your overall budget. This is going to let you keep the card but, at the same time, it's not going to completely break the bank.

Talking to Creditors

Tell them the reason why you're having a difficult time paying the debts. Most companies will negotiate a modified payment plan so monthly payments become more manageable. If you wait for the accounts to go into default, it can and most likely will affect your credit score negatively, which is what we're looking to avoid. Once in default, the collector will start calling.

CHAPTER 11:

The Importance of a Good Credit Score

Why Is Your Credit Score Important?

When you apply for credit, insurance, telephone service, and even to rent a place to live, providers want to know if you have a good level of risk. And to make that decision, they use credit scores.

A credit score is a number. A high score means you have good credit. A low score means you have bad credit. A higher score means that you represent a lower risk and that you are more likely to get the product or service — or pay less.

It works as follows: Credit grantors extract information from your credit reports, such as your bill payment history, the age of your accounts, your unpaid debts, and the collection actions initiated against you. A credit scoring system assigns points to each of the factors that serve to predict which candidates are most likely to pay a debt. The total number of points — a credit score — helps predict the odds that you will pay a loan and meet the payments by the set dates.

Credit scores can be used in various ways. These are some examples.

1. Insurance companies use the information in your credit report and also combine it with other factors to predict the level of probability that you present an insurance claim and also to predict the amount you could claim. Consider this information to decide if they will grant you insurance and how much they will charge you.

2. Public service companies use credit scores to decide if they will require a deposit from a new customer to provide the service. Cell phone providers and homeowners who rent homes also use scores when considering a new client or tenant.

3. Each type of company has different scoring systems, and credit scoring models can also be based on other information apart from the data in your credit report. For example, when you apply for a mortgage loan, the system can consider the advance, total amount of your debts, and income.

4. In order to improve your credit score in most systems, focus on paying your bills by date, cancel outstanding balances, and avoid incurring new debts.

Poor Credit vs. Good Credit

Cost of Good Credit:

They may work in the same place; they live in the same area and have similar incomes and families. The only difference between the two is their credit score.

If one maintains the good score by:

- Never max out the credit cards
- Applying for credit sparingly
- Paying bills on time
- People can get loans faster

- Credit decisions are fairer
- Credit rates are lower overall
- More credit is available

How to Convert Bad Credit to Good Credit

Nowadays, the actual worth of an individual is measured by his or her having bad credit or good credit. A person who pays all the bills on time will end up with an excellent credit rating, while a person who is casual about payments will almost always end up having bad credit. Even if he or she is able to get a loan, it will be at an extremely high-interest rate.

Hence, it is best to follow the following steps to ensure that you do not have poor bad credit or are slowly able to convert it into good credit.

1. The first and the most important thing is to pay all the bills on time, every time. Always remember that if you pay your bills more than 30 days after the last date of payment, not only is there an extra charge, but also your credit rating is spoilt.

2. All of us need to understand that the rate of interest that we pay on credit cards exceeds any other rate of interest that we may pay for any other loan. People boast of having a large number of credit cards and also pay just the minimum balance to keep the card active. This can really get you in big trouble. Hence, reduce the number of credit cards you have and try to pay the amount in full. This will help you save money and also enhance your credit ratings.

3. Avoid any kind of tax liens and bankruptcies as they are bad for credit and remain on your credit report for at least 10 years. During this time you will not be eligible for taking any loan from any bank or financial institution. This can put you in

serious trouble as it will become extremely difficult to own a vehicle or a home.

4. A number of times we get ready to become a co-borrower with a friend or a relative to help them out. Always remember that if you co-sign a particular loan, your credit history will be impacted by no payment or late payment of that particular loan. Therefore, become a co-borrower if and only if you are sure that all payments will be made on time.

It does not matter whether you have a road loan bad credit or bad mortgage credit, work towards rectifying your situation and you will be happy with the direction your life will be taking.

Starting From the Scratch and Maintaining It

How to build a credit score quickly?

It is nothing but the "score" you accumulate over time and which defines you as a good or bad debtor. I'll explain. If you have a loan of any kind, the more you pay on time and the more your Credit Score goes up; if instead, you accumulate delays or unpaid installments, your Credit Score drops one round of hell at a time (I think Dante's Inferno he referred to this when he wrote it!)

It is important that you take care of your score consistently because, over time, it will be the first thing that banks, or loan companies, will see when you ask for a loan to buy a house, a car, or anything else. At the moment, it may not seem important but trust me, you will change your mind. I've been there. I didn't give enough importance to it, and when it was time, I regretted it.

The credit card is not the prerogative of Dad's children (except for some cases), but something that young people use to start building their Credit Score from an adolescent age.

Unfortunately, we are not 16 years old, so we must try to catch up as soon as possible. The problem with the Credit Score is that it is difficult to build when you have no loans or credit cards, and it is almost impossible to get either of these if you do not have a Credit Score. In practice, a cat that bites its tail.

How to Build a Credit Score from scratch?

There are several ways and all of them are effective.

1. The first is to open a bank account. Having an account open in itself will not increase your score, but it will give you a starting point to show regular income. After a few months, you can ask your bank (remember to show off your best smile) what services they offer to increase your Credit Score. My bank, for example, offers a mini-loan of $500 tied up to be returned in 6 months. It means that you deposit $500, they re-loan them to you at a favorable rate and when, in 6 months, you finish paying the installments, they give you back the $500 in the barrel. Practically in 6 months, you paid interest as a "tax" with the sole purpose of accumulating points. To put it in simpler words: from 500 and 500 you return, then you pay 500 in installments + interest, and you return 500 at the end. It is an expense, but this type of loan guarantees you a considerable accumulation of points, but only if you are regular in payments.

2. The second, and in my opinion the best, is to apply for a Secured Credit Card. Unlike traditional credit cards, you do not have to show any kind of entry to get approval, but you also have a usage limit. The only thing required is a deposit, which is returned to you after a year of regular use. Until a couple of years ago, the deposit was around 200 euros, but with the debt problems that developed after the recession, all the major credit companies have lowered the costs. For example, I applied with Capital One (but there are many others like Discover). The deposit was only $ 49 and the card limit was $

200 a month with the option of 2% cashback on gas or restaurant expenses. I started using it regularly every month, ONLY for these two things and, after a year, my Credit Score was already considered very good, they also returned the deposit and the cashback, and the credit limit rose to 500 dollars after only six months. We clarify that you are not obliged to use it only for these things, but I have limited myself for two reasons. The first is to accumulate cashback (i.e., a refund) at the end of the year. The second is to make sure I never use more than 30% of the card limit, which brings me to the next point.

3. Never exceed 30% of the credit card limit. Believe it or not, it is essential that you show that you do not need a credit card to pay for your things, but that you use it only when strictly necessary or as an accurate choice. The more you use it constantly, the better, but judiciously.

4. Pay your installments regularly. All the above points have absolutely no value if you are not constant in payments. No one here scales your loan or credit card debts from your salary. It is your responsibility to remember when you have to pay or set up an automatic payment from your bank account. I decided to set up automatic payments. As long as he has a good memory, you never know what can happen that can put you off your mind on the expiry day. So, I strongly suggest you do the same because even a missed payment will negatively affect your score.

5. Vary the types of debt as much as you can. If you can make the Secured Card And the mini-loan with the bank at the same time, do it. The more options you have, the faster your Credit Score will grow. Of course, always keep in mind that if you don't pay on time, they show up at home with the Pit bulls (so to

speak or almost). So, if you're not sure you can do better, don't risk it and wait a little longer.

6. Add your name to someone else's credit card as an "authorized user." If, for example, you are married to an American who has had much more time than you to accumulate a decent score (as in my case), it might be a good idea for him to indicate you as an authorized user of his credit cards. This does not mean that you will actually have to use his credit cards, but the more his score improves, the more he will positively influence yours. Be careful though! If you go down, he comes down with you. This type of choice involves a fat, large demonstration of trust, so be careful not to betray it. If you mess up the Credit Score that he has been sweating so much since he was in swaddling clothes, well I wouldn't want to be in your shoes!

7. Check your Credit Score regularly to make sure there are no problems you are unaware of and have such nasty surprises. Even a late-paid bill can affect your payer profile. Now, pay attention to the following because it's important. There are several ways to check where you are with the economic 'pregnancy.' The first is to apply here for your Annual Credit Report, but you are entitled to a free check only once a year. The second is to check directly in Credit Bureaus such as Transunion, Equifax, or Experian. Also, in these cases, you can have a free check per year, or pay a monthly installment to keep your score constantly under control. Obviously, the annual checks have their advantages, but be careful not to take too much advantage of their services. Believe it or not, every time you request a check, this will lower your Credit Score. Crazy, right? And this brings me to the only sensible solution that remains to keep the score under control.

8. Download the free Credit Karma app. Not only does it constantly give you a detailed report of your score, but also what has positively or negatively influenced, which credit cards or loans are best suited to your situation, your progress, and many other functions. It's all free and, although not updated to the minute, rather accurate. It does not lower your Credit Score and also offers you many other services such as online and free tax returns. Due to Credit Karma, other major credit companies have also had to adjust to offer the Credit Score free check. For example, Capital One and Discover have now integrated this service into their offers (although in a more limited way being a cost to them).

If you follow these tips in a year, you can afford to ask for a car loan without having to pay disproportionate interest or even more, depending on your income and your general receivables/payables situation. This reminds me of how important it is to start as soon as possible. Remember that this is the first thing they look at when you need to apply for a loan!

Credit Repair: How to Improve Your Credit Score

Millions of Americans are suffering from dinged-up credit: the persistent result of the recession, the lack (until recently) of real wage increases, the slow growth of the economy. But a strong credit score is the backbone of an individual's financial health. With low or no credit, you can end up finding yourself paying a lot more for the essentials of life than those who have strong credit. The importance of a good credit score goes beyond just getting a low-interest rate on a loan. Driving credit score, for example, is an important factor in car insurance prices.

Regardless of what happened to you financially, if you have gone through foreclosure or bankruptcy, got behind on credit card payments, or collected a lot of debt, you can rebuild your credit. Here's how:

Check the Credit Report

It is determined by a series of factors that can be divided into the following categories: credit history — How long have you been using credit?

How to Apply to for Lines of Credit

You may now have high FICO scores, but that is only the beginning. At this point, it is all about knowing what to do and where to go to actually turn your credit scores into leveraged money. So, now that you have the scores that are needed, where do you go to get the money? If you just want to slowly build your credit up and you are not worried about having access to high credit limits, you can opt back in for pre-screened credit offers and apply blindly for whatever offers that may come in the mail, or you can be proactive and come up with a plan.

Going with the flow works perfectly fine for people who are not as concerned or don't take a hands-on approach to build their credit, you will stumble across some quality credit products because these offers will be sent your way, but pre-approvals don't mean you have all the necessary requirements to obtain the actual approval, and I want to save you time by getting you started in the right direction. You might have a few ideas of where you want to apply, but is it the most effective course of action? Have you developed a funding strategy yet? I have no doubt that you will receive offers for 0% balance transfers and a lot of other incentives from companies like Citi Bank, American Express, Discover, and a bunch of others, some you will actually get approved for, others will waste your time and deny you. The strategy I am going to show you will allow you to take matters into your own hands and go after what you want as far as credit limits, credit cards with benefits, and accounts that will assure you maximum future growth. You want to stay away from any credit cards that will not benefit you down the road because either they lack any substantial reward incentives or room for you to grow the credit limits. You don't want to obtain high credit limits from some, just to be held down by $500 starter credit cards from others just because you were too anxious and excited to get any approval.

Paper or Plastic

In my opinion, applying for new lines of credit is the best part of the whole process; it is more exciting than seeing your last few negative accounts falling off your credit reports. You get a rush when you get approved for lines of credit, I love the uncertainty of guessing what I will be approved for and being shocked or surprised by some lenders' generosity. Once you get deep into playing the credit game, you start to share and be exposed to information provided by others that can actually make the process fun; I advise everyone to join www.CreditBoards.com. I want everyone to know, there is no cheating, and regardless of your score, when you are in the pursuit of financing, banks lend money to those who seem to not need it, so no matter what kind of credit products you are targeting, you must keep your utilization low to stay ready. Try not to have more than 4 recent inquiries, this is the number one rule to remember when you are looking for approvals anywhere, computer underwriters can automatically deny you if you have too many recent inquiries.

I must tell you, it is almost always easier to get approved for revolving lines of credit than it is for what most may consider standard loans. I define a standard loan as a specified amount of money you may request via check from a lender, which will report as an Installment loan. For example, you might apply and ask for $10,000 and will be offered a payment term of 36 months, your payments could be around $325 per month to pay back principal and interest, just like an auto loan. Every month you know exactly what your payment is; the borrowed amount did not change and won't change unless you pay the loan off in advance. You know from the start you have a set amount of payments for a set amount of time regardless of what you do with the money. As soon as you borrow this sum, you are on the clock to repay monthly, your first payment due within the next 30 days. When most people think of getting a loan or borrowing money from a lender, they think about the standard loan product I just mentioned in the form of a check written out to them or the bank wiring the money into their bank account.

Personal Loans Are for People with Established Credit...

First, you won't get as much money as you might want if you have no prior history with paying back higher amounts of debt, specifically you will need a track record in managing revolving credit lines or other installment loans where you had access to cash; auto loans and student loans don't count for much. It is a big misconception that student loans and auto loans can build your credit for you, that concept and theory are only half true.

As I have mentioned before, it is easy to borrow a large amount of money for school without having any real credit; you have to understand the logic which determines the risk of unsecured loans versus the safety behind secured or insured loans. Most student loan products are insured by the government to benefit the lender and you will be forced to pay the loan back with interest, no matter if you finish school or not. Buying a car and getting approved for an auto loan isn't a hard task either; the lender's investment is secured, as the vehicle is the collateral in the event of default.

For example, as a first-time buyer with no history of making any car payments or any other loan payments, you can get approved for a loan with minimum credit history to buy a car for $30,000 or even more, do you think they would loan you that much cash as a personal loan? The answer is no, you have some building to do. You might sustain a decent credit score with only a student loan or auto loan reporting positively on your credit reports, but you will not provide much of a track record to show and prove to banks that you are a reliable borrow. You will need credit card history to accomplish this.

Banks are not foolish, most lenders are very careful not to loan out significant amounts of cash to borrowers for personal use. They already calculated your spending habits before you even applied, they know what neighborhoods you live in, how much money everyone in your zip code makes, they know how long you lived at your current address, and they can even determine your level of education; If you think I am joking, take a look at some of your specialty consumer reports, take note of all of the information that is kept on you. Remember, on every application, you will fill out, you have no choice but to submit your address, and that is all they will need to determine how much of a risk you are.

How to Graduate Credit Card Levels...

Just like everything in life, you have levels and systems in place that you have no choice but to follow. You can't start kindergarten, then go directly to college just because you are in a rush to grow up. You have to take your time to go from one level to the next, and when it comes to credit, here is a broad example of how the credit card system is layered.

- LEVEL 1 ($200–$1,000): This is your entry-level into the credit card world. The basic subprime credit cards, store cards, or secured credit cards offered to people with no credit or bad credit, make sure any credit card you get reports to all 3 major credit bureaus or it is a waste of effort. Some people can get approved for a Capital One Platinum credit card with little to no credit, if not, Capital One will ask for a partial deposit for their secured credit card if you have no prior history at all. Credit cards included at this level are Capital One Platinum, Credit One, First Premier, Open Sky, Finger-Hut, and Self-Lender. I always advise people to stay away from any starter credit card that requires an annual fee unless they have no other choice. Keep in mind, you can apply for store cards like Kohl's, Lowes, Toys R Us, and Victoria Secret just to build credit, but unless you are a loyal customer and shop there every month, I would advise you to stay away from getting more than one store credit card until you are established, they are frowned upon by prime banks and can delay you later on. In the credit world, store credit cards are considered "toy cards." Stick to credit cards you can use everywhere that have Visa, MasterCard, Discover, or American Express logos. Store credit cards are only good for that specific retailer. You only need 1 starter credit card, but more will not hurt, don't be greedy and get more than 3 unless they are cards that can graduate.

- LEVEL 2 ($1,000–$4,500): At this level, you can consider your credit as being healthy; you are in a good position to build. Be very careful to manage your accounts so you don't miss any payments and your balances are low. At Level 2 you are being watched carefully by your creditors and will receive automatic credit line increases periodically with good borrowing behavior. Don't fall for the subprime credit offers from banks and companies you have never even heard of at this point. Regardless of your score, more than likely you still have a thin file and will be denied for a lot of other pre-approvals from prime banks. Credit Cards including in this level are Discover It, Chase Freedom, Chase Slate, Capital One Quicksilver, American Express Blue Cash Everyday, and Citi Double Cash. Be very careful not to overdo it at this point, you are more focused on quality and not quantity. You should only accept and apply for prime banks and creditors as listed above, you will be able to use these cards to add authorized users of your choice, these accounts will help you build strong credit lines later. I strongly suggest Capital One starter cards at levels 1 and 2 as you can convert their products into more desirable credit cards for growth and rewards like the Quicksilver or Venture credit cards.

• LEVEL 3 ($5,000–$10,000): Now, you have reached the ideal time to go for big money credit lines. Level 3 shows that you have very strong primary credit cards, big limits beget other big limits, you can organically grow your accounts at this point with periodic credit line increases as some lenders will try to match the credit limits of current creditors, not Barclay, they are followers, they don't like to be the lowest credit limit and do not like to be the highest either, they also ignore the credit limits you get from credit unions. With decent primary tradelines reporting at these mentioned credit limits, it is very easy to blend in authorized users accounts to take your credit to the next level. Most cards from level 2 will graduate within 3–6 months to this level if you are responsible. Credit card issuers like Chase, Barclay American Express, and Bank of America will actually allow you to combine 2 separate credits cards that are issued by them, this strategy will allow you to get to a higher credit limit. Think about it, you have 1 card with a $3,500 limit and another with $4,500 from the same issuer, you can request that the cards be combined; I suggest you keep the oldest card open. After you combine the limits, you can periodically ask for credit limit increases (CLI's).

Keep in mind that Chase will automatically deny most applicants who have 5 new credit accounts that have been opened in the past 24 months. If you are going to apply for Chase, I suggest you do it at the beginning of your first application spree. At this point, you should get an American Express Blue Cash credit card if you haven't already. You can get a 3x credit limit increase after 61 days, and another 3x credit limit increase after 6 months. That means you can go from $1,000 to $3,000, then from $3,000 to $9,000 within only 6 months. Applying at credit unions can be very helpful in getting you your first $10,000 credit card, I recommend Navy Federal, if you are eligible, you must have someone who has a member access number, you must be affiliated to someone in the military. With only 1 or 2 primaries and 1 aged AU, you can get approvals for $10,000 & up very easily. Hundreds of different credit unions can be used to get you high-limit credit approvals, especially Navy Federal, NASA, Pen-Fed, Alliant, and Digital Credit Union. You will also get the best interest rates for auto loans at a credit union.

- LEVEL 4 ($15,000–$20,000): This is where you want to be and the opportunities will easily come your way. Your mailbox will be full of offers from the best credit card companies. With any high-limit primary credit card reporting in this range, you should be able to secure 3 additional cards in the 5-figure range after paying on this primary for 90 days. Once you get any primary account of your own to report for only a few months, it will help you get approved for others. High limits will get lenders competing for your usage.

Let's say you start off with Navy Federal, you apply for 1 credit card and a not so ambitious personal loan of only $7,000–

$9,000 at the same time, this is just to build the relationship. Navy federal will approve you for more credit than you currently have reported by any other creditor, and possibly surpass your highest credit limit by $5,000.

*You should get at least 3 credit cards from major issuers within your first 6–9 months of building. The help of authorized user tradelines will increase your ability to reach level 4 within your first year. I recommend you get American Express Platinum, Chase Sapphire Reserve, Chase Marriot, Capital One Venture, Barclay Arrival, and let them grow at this point. All of these cards can graduate, your limits can start at $10,000 and go up to $50,000 or more, you can apply and be approved for multiple credit cards from the same lenders if you develop a good relationship.

- LEVEL 5 ($30,000–$50,000+): You have reached the promised land. At this level, you can enjoy the highest benefits offered by creditors as you have aged your credit file, proved yourself responsible, and manage to build a thick file. Getting any credit card to the $50,000 range will put you at the maximum exposure for most creditors, depending on income. If you have a good relationship with American Express and used their Platinum card, you might even get a Black Card invitation. Some say that Black Card holders need an income of $1 million or more to get the invitation, but if you spend enough money, I'm sure they would love to have you in their Black Card family. You can focus on building the credit limits for all of your credit cards once you have any credit card a limit over $20,000 to provoke other issuers to follow the leader. Discover, Citi Bank, and Wells Fargo seems to be stingy, so don't get your hopes up.

CHAPTER 12:

Your Financial Freedom

Financial freedom is a concept that people love to think about but rarely feel like they can reach. This chapter will help you reach financial freedom by using tips and habits that can be incorporated into your life.

What Is Meant by Financial Freedom?

Financial freedom has no set definition. However, it typically means that you are living comfortably, saving for retirement and in general. It can also mean that you have an emergency reserve set up. In general, financial freedom can mean whatever you want it to mean for you. For example, a prior college student may not think that financial freedom includes paying off all their student loans. This is because, at least in this day and age, a college student who needs to pay their own way realizes they will always be paying off their student loans. However, they might feel that student loans are the only debt they should have. Therefore, being able to pay off credit cards or medical bills leads them to financial freedom.

Some people might feel that financial freedom indicates they have absolutely no debt or loans. This includes them having paid off their mortgage and any car loans. They might also feel that in order to reach financial freedom, they need to be investing in a CD, bond, or even in the stock market.

Other people may feel that financial freedom means they are no longer tied down to a job. They are able to live off of their savings or a passive income, and they are able to retire and enjoy life through traveling.

Credit Cards and Financial Freedom - Is It Safe?

One of the biggest questions people have when it comes to financial freedom is whether they can have any credit card accounts in their name. While you may not owe anything on your credit cards (in fact, you might only owe one which you pay off in full every month), is this still financial freedom? In general, this is completely determined by your definition of financial freedom. However, if you ever find yourself not being able to pay off your credit card every month, this is not financial freedom. In most cases, financial freedom does mean you no longer have any debt, or at least that you are free from unnecessary debt, such as credit cards.

Most people are quick to state that financial freedom and credit cards do not go together simply because they are not safe with each other. This is due to the fact that it is often easy to fall back into thinking you can pay the amount off everything each month, and then you become unable to do so. In general, people who reach financial freedom feel that credit cards allow for more of a trap and keep them from ever reaching financial freedom.

However, other people who feel they have reached financial freedom state that as long as you can manage your credit cards wisely, they can be included with your freedom. Some of them also advise that you set up a financial freedom plan. Within this plan, you will state your conditions for using a credit card. Of course, you need to be self-disciplined enough to follow your condition.

The Best Habits to Help You Reach and Protect Your Financial Freedom

When it comes to financial freedom, there are dozens of habits and tips that people provide in order to help you reach your financial freedom. It is important to note that because financial freedom can vary depending on the person's definition, some of the tips and habits might work for you while others may not. You need to find the ones that work best for you, not the ones that other people say are the best. Therefore, I am going to give you a fairly large list as I want you to make sure that you can find some of the best habits and tips, so you can not only reach financial freedom but also protect it.

Make a Budget

Making and keeping a budget is one of the first steps everyone should take while heading towards financial freedom. Even though you might find yourself changing your budget now and then, as you will add or delete bills or receive a different income, you always want to follow it. Not only will this help you in reaching your financial freedom, but continuing to follow your budget will also protect your financial freedom.

Furthermore, creating a monthly budget can make sure that all your bills are being paid and you know exactly where your money is going. For example, you will be able to see how much money you spend on groceries, gas, and eating out at restaurants. This will help you know where you can decrease your spending, which will allow you to save more. There are a lot of great benefits when it comes to creating and sticking with a household budget.

Set Up Automatic Savings Account

If you work for an organization that will automatically place a certain percentage of your check into a savings account, take advantage of this. It gives you the idea that you never had the money to begin with, which means you don't plan for it and you won't find yourself taking the money out of savings unless you need it for an emergency. Furthermore, you can set up a separate savings account where this money will go. You can make it so you rarely see this account; however, you want to make sure that your money is deposited and everything looks right on your account. But, the point of this account is that you do not touch it, even if you have an emergency. Instead, you will set up a different account for an emergency basis.

The other idea to this is you pay yourself first. This is often something that people don't think about because they are more worried about paying off their debt. However, many financial advisors say that you are always number one when it comes to your finances. While you want to pay your bills, you also need to make sure that you and your family are taken care of.

Keep Your Credit in Mind without Obsessing Over It

Your credit score is important, but it is not the most important thing in the world. People often fall into the trap of becoming obsessed over their credit score, especially when they are trying to improve it. One factor to remember is that your credit score is typically only updated every so often. Therefore, you can decide to set time aside every quarter to check on your credit report. When you do this, you not only want to check your score, but you also want to check what the credit bureaus are reporting. Just like you want to make sure everything is correct on your bank account, you want to do the same thing for your credit report.

It Is Fine to Live Below Your Means

One of the biggest factors of financial freedom and being able to maintain it is you can make your bills and comfortably live throughout the month. In order to do this, you need to make sure that the money coming into your home is more than the money going out. In other words, you want to live below your means.

This is often difficult for a lot of people because they want to have what other people have. They want to have the newer vehicles, the bigger boat, the newest grill, or anything else. People like to have what their friends and neighbors have. However, one factor people don't think about is that their friends and neighbors probably don't have financial freedom. Therefore, you want to take a moment to think about what is more important for you. Would you rather be in debt like your friends, or would you rather have financial freedom?

Speak With a Financial Advisor

Sometimes, the best step we can take when working towards financial freedom is talking with a financial advisor. They can often give up information, help us with a budget, make sure that we get the most out of our income, and tell us where we might be spending more money than we should. Furthermore, they can help you figure out what the best investments are, which are always helpful when you are looking at financial freedom. At the same time, they can help you plan for your retirement, which is one of the biggest ways you will be able to remain financially free.

Completely Pay Off Your Credit Cards

If you have high-interest credit cards, which is often the case, you want to make sure that you pay these off every month. Therefore, your credit card spending should become part of your budget. What this means is you don't want to use your credit card for whatever you feel like. Instead, you want to create a list of when you can and when you can't use your credit card. For example, you might agree that it is fine in emergency situations or during Christmas shopping. You might also feel that you can use it during tip because it has trip insurance attached to it. Whatever you decide, you want to make sure you follow.

You also want to make sure that you pay off any high-interest loans. When it comes to loans that are lower in interest, they won't affect you too much.

Track Your Spending

Along with making sure you follow your budget, you also want to track your spending. There are several reasons for this. First, it will help you make sure that your budget is on track. We often forget about automatic bills that are paid monthly or don't realize how much we really spend every month. These factors can make our budget off, which can cause an obstacle when you are working to reaching and keeping your financial freedom.

Fortunately, there are a lot of apps that you can download, many of them are free, which will allow you to easily track your spending. Some of these apps include Mint or Personal Capital. These apps typically give you all the information you need and will automatically tell you how much you are spending and how much income you still hold at the end of the month. Most of these apps will also give you charts to help you see your spending habits in a different way.

Continue Your Education

Another way to stay on top of your financial freedom is to become educated when it comes to your budget, spending, taxes, and anything else to do with your finances. This doesn't mean that you have to go back to school and earn a degree. You can simply do your own research or take online classes, some of which you will find are low-cost to free. You can also look into webinars that people hold.

You can also help yourself when it comes to investing in the stock market or anything else. There are always several classes you can take online which only have a few sessions or ways you can learn when you have the time. In fact, if you want to invest but don't know what to do or where to begin, one of your best options is to take a class.

Make Sure to Keep Your Mindset

This is a mindset that you will want to continue to have while you are living financially free. With this mindset, you will not only feel grateful for where you are in life, but you will also remember where you once were. This will help you work towards protecting your financial freedom instead of falling back into credit card debt.

Of course, you can adjust your mindset the way you want to once you reach financial freedom. However, you will want to make sure that you keep your mindset positive. After all, a positive mindset makes you believe that you can accomplish anything.

Make Sure You Write down What Financial Freedom Means to You

As stated before, financial freedom can mean something different to you than it means to someone else. Because of this, you have to think about what it truly means to you. Whatever you feel it means, it is important to write this down. This will allow you to turn back to what financial freedom means to you when you find yourself struggling and feeling like you can't gain your financial freedom.

At the same time, it is also helpful to take time to write down your goals. Think of what you want to accomplish on your road to financial freedom. You can also think about what you want to do after you have reached financial freedom. Give yourself goals to work towards as this will help you stay on track better.

Conclusion

So far in this wonderful exposition, I have unveiled the core truths about credit and creditworthiness, and we have discussed the most vital strategies by which you can repair your credit and boost your credit score from bad to excellent all by yourself. However, it is important not to get so carried away in your desperation to repair your credit that you begin to indulge in the most common errors which may ultimately sabotage your efforts. As a takeaway package, I present to you some of the most salient mistakes to watch against as you repair your credit. From my encounter with people in your shoes who have one difficulty or the other with their credit history, these mistakes are both common and subtle. As a matter of fact, some of them seem to be solutions or hacks in credit repair, but they ultimately undo your efforts. Get your highlighter ready!

Failure to Check Credit Reports

This is perhaps the most foundational problem in credit repair. It stems from stark ignorance or mere recklessness, or a poor finance-related habit or the intentional refusal to face the facts of your credit status. Well, the truth is that the refusal to own up to your credit mess doesn't take it away. The reality will come haunting you the moment you step into a bank to request a loan, or you need to apply for a new job and the employer requests it! Regularly checking your credit report keeps you updated with your credit status and helps you identify problem areas to thrash out. It also keeps you abreast with the specific areas where your report is being negatively affected, what information to address or dispute, and what part of your financial involvements to focus on. As far as credit is concerned, the more you know, the better your credit status. More so, bear in mind that it is a great disservice to yourself to wait till a financial firm or employer requests your credit reports before you check them up yourself. There are several known online platforms to check your reports. A typical example is the Federal Trade Commission Free Credits Report page.

Failure to Pay Down Debt Quickly

What many do not realize is that paying off your debts, and quickly too, is one of the most assured ways to remedy your bad credit. The way out is to offset your debts in small regular bits. Staying true to a particular pattern of debt clearance greatly improves your credit score. Take down credits seriously, especially the credit cards that are close to being maxed out. Another similarly significant approach is to pay your installment loans such as student loans and auto loans, depending on which ones apply to you. Constantly reducing your loans and debts does not only improve your credit score but sells you as a dependable and responsible client to future employers, loan firms, banks, and other finance-related organizations.

Improper or No Documentation

Documentation is highly essential to arriving at an awesome credit score. It is wrong to fail to take documentation of every financial activity you engage in. Your spending history is one of the factors put into consideration by credit bureaus to calculate your credit score. This explains why you should never agree to an oral agreement; however flimsy it seems. All payments should be backed with paperwork or at least receipts. In as much as there is a financial commitment attached to it, ensure you have it properly documented. Your documented payments and financial activities come in handy when or if you have a reason to dispute a report later in the future. Bureaus do not work with oral agreements, so if you have been offsetting a debt or repaying a loan, for example, ensure it is well documented.

Excessive Disputes

Mistakes are inevitable in credit reports. Most times, they are the consequences of insufficient information, which may be caused by improper documentation as mentioned above. When you notice an error in your report, it is only normal to react by filing a dispute. However, filing excessive disputes will do quite the opposite to your credit reports. More so, it is wrong to dispute the entire report. You should dispute only information you are sure about, and you have adequate backup or evidence to prove.

Filing for Bankruptcy

Filing for bankruptcy is a rather delicate credit repair approach you should use with caution because it never really helps your credit. Of course, it temporarily liberates you from the debt load and makes you focus on other productive financial commitments, you must bear in mind that bankruptcy never really works without affecting your future creditworthiness. It leaves a taint on your credit. File for bankruptcy today, and it remains glued to your credit history for at least seven to ten years, thereby holding the likelihood of impeding a future loan.

Transferring Credit Card Balances

Sometimes, credit repair experts and companies suggest transferring credit balances from card to card as a credit repair technique, but this is always not a good idea. It does not reduce nor take away the number of debts you owe. More so, you will still have to sacrifice your interests because most times, the transfer fees overshadow whatever interests you might get.

Some people do this because they want to close the other credit cards and consolidate their debts onto one single credit card. In the end, you lose more than you gain. You sacrifice the credit history you have so far garnered on the credit cards you wish to close.

Canceling Credit Card Accounts

Is this really a good idea? Maybe not! You can never increase your credit score by closing your credit cards. The truth about your credit report, as you have learned so far, is that there are so many factors in place. Closing a credit card account with many bad records such as debts, late payments, and so on, seems to be able to boost your credit score, but on the contrary, that is not so. This is because the length of your credit history is one of the major factors that inputs your credit report. Closing an account does nothing but reduce the length of your credit card history, thereby making you lose some points in that regard. The most vital way out is to keep the accounts and reduce the low payments on them.

Getting Back into Bad Debts

Bad debts are quick ways to lose points on your credit score. It is normal and even recommended to secure a loan for a business activity that will yield much more than the loan and the interests put together. That is good debt, but anything contrary is bad debt. Bad debts leave you frustrated and leave your credit score affected. After clearing off debt, many individuals and small corporations often go back into debt in a bid to raise enough funds for their business activities and engagements. While this isn't an entirely bad idea, what is bad about it is the nature of loans they have acquired and the terms involved, which often results in debts that are difficult to pay. Unfortunately, too many bad debts sabotage your efforts to build both your business and your credit score.

Hiring a Shady Credit Repair Company

Although hiring a credit repair company or expert isn't a bad idea for people who do not have the expertise or patience to undertake the process involved in repairing or fixing a bad credit score, it comes with its own disadvantages and cost. Most credit repair companies, in a bid to impress their clients, blindly dispute credit reports. This is often the first step towards failure. At the end of the day, much positive information is removed from the client's records. Another major downside to hiring credit repair companies is the cost involved. According to Credit Karma, service charges of such companies range from about $50 to $150 on a monthly basis for services you could render yourself with a few tips and patience.

www.ingramcontent.com/pod-product-compliance
Lightning Source LLC
Chambersburg PA
CBHW071420210526
45465CB00001B/473